Forty Days of Bullseyes

Growing up in Dublin Ireland

D M Weir

Cover Sketch of 100 Lower Clanbrassil Street by
Brian Donnelly
Courtesy of Gerald Donnelly

Lulu.com

Forty Days of Bullseyes

© D M Weir 2008

ISBN 978-1- 4092-3691-7

**I dedicate this Book to my children, Sylvius, Tonya and Clara
And to my grandchildren Holly, Leo and Alex**

Acknowledgements

A vote of thanks to my brothers Ciaran and Gerald. My sisters Aileen, Nuala, Myra, Enda and Rachel. My sisters-in-law, Sheila (Brian's wife) Judy (Terry's wife)and Doris (Pearse's wife), for their individual contributions in adding humour and personal reminiscences. Also to my friends Theresa Moran, Noeleen Urell and Ann Field for being helpful in putting names to people and places, Rita O'Rourke(Betty & Stella's friend)and to my cousin Frances Carrick and Betty Gorman a school friend.

Thanks to my readers, Sophia Joyce, Sara Nesbitt and Rita Crick, who read my story first, hot off the press (or should I say, computer) and gave me positive feedback, and special thanks to Mike Crowson, a fellow author for his expertise in putting it all together, for without you all this book would not have come this far!

Chapter 1

Born in 1943

I was not born with a Silver Spoon in me mouth. No-one gave me a Silver Christening Cup, or a Silver Egg Cup and Spoon, or even Silver Tooth and Curl Boxes. Our Street did not have places with names like La Senza, La Tasca or Organic Planet. Gucci shoes or Reebok Trainers had not yet become the 'In Thing' to wear and Designer Clothes were only for the rich and famous from Shops like Cassidy's, Brown Thomas' and Switzers' and me mammy was not 'Too Posh to Push'.

The year being 1943. Was it a good year? You ask! Well, maybe for some but for me mammy it would mean an extra mouth to feed, an up and coming toddler under her feet and more nappies to wash but it was summer, so maybe dry weather outside might have helped.

The newspaper headlines read 'More towns fall to the Allies'. Advance continues in Sicily. Palermo is claimed to be in Allied hands. Talks being held at The Trades Union Congress on Irish Aid for War Refugees, and the healthy state of the brown trout!. Closer on the home front in Dublin city another child enters the world, I was the first child to be born into the family after the death of me granddaddy Leo Augustine Donnelly who had died on December 15th 1942. Before the memorable day of my arrival I was but a 'Twinkle in me daddy's eye'. I weighed in at eight pounds, with a very pale complexion and a head of dark brown hair.

Me grand entrance day was Saturday July 24$^{th.}$ 10.45am. The weather forecast predicted another sweltering hot day. All sun worshipers, families and swimmers alike were spilling on to overflowing trains arriving on platforms in Amiens Street, Tara Street, Westland Row and Harcourt Street railway stations to carry them to their favourite beaches, to savour the refreshing cool breezes that they hoped were coming off the coast as the call of the sea waters beckoned them to Sandymount, Booterstown, Blackrock, Seapoint, Killiney, Bray, Greystones and beyond on Dublin's South Coast, and to Dollymount, Portmarnock, Malahide and as far as Howth on Dublin's North Coast.

While the staff in Hollis Street Maternity Hospital, Dublin at approximately 10.45am helped the fifth twinkle make it's way into the world, that was me!. They tell me I wasn't too anxious to be born and was willing meself to remain in that safe place if it had been at all possible. Another daughter to Leo and Rachel Donnelly nee Cullinan.

As me head emerged I could feel the heat, but it was a different heat. Me eyes were closed but the bright lights were burning the delicate skin of me eyelids trying to penetrate them as though saying to me, 'Come on, open your eyes, you have arrived!', but I wasn't ready to open me eyes and I didn't. The voices sounded so loud and urgent in me little ears. Then followed strange noises and sounds, not the muffled ones I had become accustomed to and could sleep through. It was as though there was an urgency, as unseen shadows moved around following commands and demands. I had left behind me that protected and cushioned world. Life as I knew it, nine months of security, warmth, ready nourishment and quietness was over.

That choice was gone forever when the rest of me floated out on that last push and I was separated from me mammy. Someone was making sure I was of this new world when I took me first breath and let them know with a loud protest that I was not happy. This then was the first time I would have been held in a real person's hands as I was being wrapped in a warm blanket. Me greatest need at that moment was for a drink, something warm and soothing. When that wish took so long in being fulfilled I resigned meself to the fact that for some reason or other 'Life was going to be an uphill battle from then on and, this was before I would get the news that I was not going to have the privilege of being a pampered only child with all me worldly wishes fulfilled instantly!

....

Chapter 2

Hospital Visiting

At the early age of four days old I sensed something different in the ward. Visiting hours seemed to have changed. Yes, me aunts and uncles and granny and lots of people turned up to see me mammy but more importantly to see me. I couldn't really see them, they were still only mere shadows to me, but I could hear them laughing and they seem to be happy and I felt meself being lifting into the air and they were making very strange sounds, I was being hugged and kissed and passed around to everyone that was visiting. It felt very nice, I wanted more!.

Then the strangest thing happened that I couldn't understand. I'd had a bath earlier and I was dressed, now they were undressing me and then they were dressing me again! This time (I was told later) I was dressed in the family Christening robe that had been worn by me daddy, who was the eldest in his family, his brother Pearse, his sisters Evelyn, Betty, Stella, me own two sisters and two brothers, not forgetting many of me granny's neighbour's children as well. Sounded like the gown had been around a while!. It was a long white garment, very soft to the touch with lots of delicate lace interlinked with cotton, a lace bodice top with a tiny lace collar and lace sleeves, then everyone around was oo..ing and ah..ing and isn't she gorgeous. I was carried the short distance to the Parish Church of St. Andrew's, Westland Row to be Baptised, me Auntie Stella, was to be me God-mother, and the visitors came too.

....

Chapter 3

Baptism and What Name?

At me Baptism I was given the names Deirdre Monica. Now Irish parents are renowned for naming their children after either Saints or names connected with Folklore Irish legends and in my case, A Folklore Legend!.
 This is the story of me namesake, ©'Deirdre and the Sons of Uisneach'. Deirdre was born of the Royal Scanchai, Fedlimid. The druid Cathbad, announced that he had heard Deirdre cry in the womb before she was born and he predicted that she would grow to be a beautiful woman whom men would fight over but that she would bring ruin upon Ulster. King Conor Mac Nessa announced he would marry her himself when she became a woman. Now, King Conor Mac Nessa was taking no chances of anyone else seeing her so he made sure she led a sheltered life in a cottage in the woods under the watchful eye of a governess named Leabharcham. As with all true legends, against all the odds, nature will take it's course so when Deirdre had grown into a young and beautiful woman as predicted, she saw the handsome Red Branch Knights, Ainle, Ardan and Naoise who were brothers, she fell in love with Naoise.
 It wasn't long before King Connor heard about this and was infuriated. Naoise carried Deirdre away from Ulster with his brothers acting as bodyguards for protection. They roamed from kingdom to kingdom because King Connor was in pursuit and wanted Deirdre for himself. Then the King of Alba, the Scottish King heard about her beauty and also made plans to have her for himself. So while the two kings were making their own plans to kidnap her she had a dream and saw a halo of blood around Naoise's head and begged him to take her to Cuchullain's home in Dundalk. On their way they met Leabharcham who hid Deirdre in a fortress.
 Naoise couldn't keep away from Deirdre, he loved her too much. On one of Naoise's secret visits to her he was followed and her whereabouts was discovered. As Naoise and his brothers went out riding they were attacked and all sorts of sorcery was used eventually lead to their deaths. Deirdre was broken-hearted and refused to be comforted. She saw no reason to live. She was so distraught she killed herself. They say she died of a broken heart. Since then Chroniclers have called her

'Deirdre of the Sorrows'. A name with a legend for a baby!

Me mammy didn't come with me to see me being Baptised. That was quite normal for a baby's mammy not to be at her child's baptism then. If a baby was of a delicate nature or there was possible reason that a baby might die within the first weeks of it's life, a person, and not necessarily a priest, could perform a Baptism on the child with ordinary tap water until holy water could be found. That rite was called 'Conditional Baptism'. This ceremony would prevent the un-baptised child going into 'Limbo' where babies, Holy Innocents, as they were called, went because they still had 'Original Sin' - the sin of Adam & Eve on their souls. I was definitely not going to be visiting 'Limbo'. After the ceremony I was brought back to the hospital to be with me mammy who was recovering from pneumonia, the doctors had advised against her going home too soon.

....

©Taken from Ancient Irish Legends by Padraic O'Farrell. 1995
Published by Gill & Macmillan

Chapter 4

Being Introduced to me Brothers and Sisters
Auntie Essie moves out

When me mammy was well enough to go home she brought me home to meet 'The other twinkles in me daddy's eye', me brothers and sisters, Aileen six yrs old, Brian five, Terry three and Nuala nearly two.

Home was a two bed roomed house at 100 Lower Clanbrassil Street, Dublin 8. Clanbrassil Street was nicknamed 'Little Jerusalem', as most of the people who lived, worked, owned shops or earned a living on that street, especially those living towards Leonard's Corner and the South Circular Road were mostly Jewish. They worshiped at their Synagogue in Lombard Street. Our family attended Mass at St. Teresa's Catholic Church near Fatima Mansions, Donore, during our early years because our granny and aunts and uncle lived in O'Donovan Road (which was on the way) even though our Parish was St. Kevin's Church, Harrington Street.

Me bed was the bottom drawer from the tallboy that stood in the front bedroom, until I was big enough to take me turn in the cot in the corner. The front bedroom, which overlooked the main street, was the only bedroom for everyone to sleep in. The family was still young.

When me daddy and mammy got married they had a small flat on Emorville Avenue which was only big enough for the two of them but not big enough for a family that was growing as the years went by, Me daddy's Aunt Essie and her brother Frank were living in the Clanbrassil Street house. When Aunt Essie realized nieces and nephews were arriving at a steady pace she decided she would move in with her sister Mary on Albans Road. Uncle Frank who had remained a bachelor decided to stay behind in the house in Clanbrassil Street and turned the back bedroom upstairs into his own living space. They tell me he seemed to enjoy the sound of us children in the house, that he was also very kind and the family in turn loved him being around.

It was a very old house and believed to have been condemned even before the family came to live there. They said the house was over a hundred years old, that seemed very old!. Downstairs there was a long hall with a door leading off for the front parlour, that room was rented to a young couple with a baby for about two years. Next to the parlour was a door leading into a large kitchen, the warmest room in the house during the cold wet winter months. There was no central heating and there wouldn't ever be while we lived there so the warmth of the house depended on heat from the black range in the kitchen and the fire being lit. There was always water boiling on the range. The kitchen was the only room down stairs for everyone to share. Then down a short passage was a scullery with a cold water tap and a very deep square porcelain sink to wash in but if anything was dropped by accident it just smashed into bits. The scullery had a door leading to the backyard and a window looking out to it over the sink. Then there was the toilet. It was indoors but seemed to be forever without a light bulb so the door had to be kept opened a fraction. The house was one of a block of four.

Our neighbours next door at 101 were Mr and Mrs Halpin, a very kind and friendly couple who hadn't children of their own but seemed to have many visitors and usually a bike propped against their front window railing. They kept a keen interest in all that we did. They never complained about the noise which must have been horrendous. Running up and down the stairs or jumping them two by two, sliding down the banisters, in and out of the scullery, sliding in the hall, the front door and every other door being constantly slammed, not forgetting the fighting and crying that took place. There were no angels living there, just normal children. The younger they were the noisier they were and they just kept coming.

At number 102 lived Mrs. Grace and then at number 103 our last neighbours were Mr. and Mrs. Syney who lived in the red brick house on the corner.

....

Chapter 5

Six Months old and Hospital Visits

Life went on as usual in our house and I began to thrive, like most babies who are breast fed. They tell me I was about six months old when I started to lose weight and nobody could fathom out why or what was causing it especially as everyone else in the family seemed healthy enough. So began the hospital visits which were the start of a very miserable time of crying and discomfort and family upset.

After constant visits to Harcourt St. Children's hospital it was agreed by the doctors that the problem seemed to have started when I'd been started on solid food. Baby food such as baby biscuits (rusks) mixed with milk seemed harmless enough and usually babies thrived on it and it helped fill them up and they would sleep happily through the night, but it wasn't to be like that for me.

Life was taking a downward spiral. What was going to happen? Me tummy was becoming rock hard and I was showing signs of being starved. Because I was too young to understand any of this I cried a lot. So while Farley's Baby Rusks normally made the life of a baby 'happy and bouncy' it was having the opposite effect on me. I was diagnosed as suffering from an allergy but it would be one or two years before 'the allergy' would be given a name. It was the beginning of a long, painful and unhappy relationship between me and me mammy and doctors, nurses and hospital visits.

Harcourt Street Hospital for sick children began to play a prominent and a very fearful unhappy part in me life. Every hospital visit was a trauma. Me body became a showpiece for visiting students and doctors interested in me condition. Coeliac disease was finally diagnosed. So there I was stood naked on a bed, everyone standing around talking and looking as though I wasn't there. It wasn't a time where there were private rooms either, just curtains. As I got older I was aware of all those children's eyes on the other side of the curtains peering in. Then followed a blood test taken from me finger, which made me cry as well, it didn't take much to make me cry. Each visit to the clinic in Harcourt Street Hospital outpatients department ended with me mammy armed with bags weighing down the pram filled with pint sized glass bottles full of iron tonic with rubber stoppers, and returnable for refills, (no refunds!) and a follow up appointment. The smell of the dispensary, in which we seemed to have been kept waiting for hours, remained in our nostrils long after we had left.

....

Chapter 6

Unhappy Experiences in Harcourt Street Hospital.

It's hard to say how young I was but I was constantly aware I was different from the rest of the family and not allowed to eat most things everyone else could.

"No, you can't eat that but you can have this" and the 'this' was exactly what I didn't like and definitely didn't want. Happy memories stay within for a long time but unhappy times seem to take a hold, wrap themselves into our very core and stay longer. They become strong memories and the many stays in hospital created many unhappy nightmares and fears.

Hospitals and even children's hospitals weren't overly child friendly in the 1940s. It was an alien world to a child who was part of a young family, with lots of child friendly people around and then to be thrust into a world of strangers. Rows of beds. No family around. Just scurrying nurses too busy to have time to console a newcomer. It was a frightening world of stiff sheets and enamel dishes, not something a sick child would be used to at home. Strange faces everywhere, too much time on their own, feeling lost and abandoned. It was a strange and frightening world of medicine that didn't taste nice or smell nice and big needles into baby flesh.

It was a world of strict visiting hours but no visitors for me. I had to learn the art of waiting for someone who wouldn't be coming. An expectant look of anticipation that wouldn't be fulfilled. The long hours with that sick feeling of unexplained fear caught up inside waiting, forever waiting for something horrible to happen.

I recall one time I was in a small ward with only three other babies who were asleep. The blinds were pulled down and the lights turned low and I cried and was afraid and lonely. From the moment I was put in a cot I cried and cried, frightened of everything and everyone. Any time I saw a man wearing a white-coat, even if he was just walking past and wasn't even in the ward or room I became hysterical and caused meself to become worse.

There was an occasion two nurses came into the ward where I had been sitting quietly looking out the window on to the street. I had tubes up me nose going to me tummy but I was perfectly happy. One of the nurses put a treatment tray of instruments with a white cover over it on me bed making me think they were going to do something to me. I sat there and began crying until I was beginning to feel sick.

The nurses then let down the side of the cot next to me to change a dressing on that baby. One nurse took the tray off me bed, looked at me and they both laughed. It took me a long time to stop crying as the tears dripped off me chin and I had a snotty nose. I was even slapped once because I said I hadn't had any dinner when one of the other nurses said I had!.

As I got older they started giving injections in the top of me legs every day, which made me cry all the more. I was also given a variety of tonics during me long stays, some iron and virol. The virol tasted like toffee and it took away the taste of the iron, yuk!. I was also given tablets to take: now that didn't seem quite right and the tablets ended up in a stuffed fish that had a little hole near the fin.

Hospital stays were not good for me health as I was continually distressed and frightened and I was definitely sick with temper at the least upset, so when me paper bag of dolly mixture sweets were taken from me and eaten by the nurses. Oh, how I hated everybody!.

And one other unhappy incident comes to mind. During what could only have been my last stay in Harcourt Street Hospital, or should have been, I was put in a ward with ten other children and again I had a bed by the window looking out onto the traffic on Harcourt Street so I could be distracted by people, cars and buses going by and away from what was going on in the ward. I was happier there with the distractions.

I didn't cry so much anymore, well that was until on a sunny afternoon when I was day-dreaming and enjoying meself looking out the window when I spied me mammy pushing a pram with a baby in it, me sister Nuala and me brother Terry skipping along holding on to the pram, I presumed they were on their way to St. Stephen's Green which just happened to be down the road from the hospital. I couldn't see who was in the pram but I knew they weren't coming to see me. They didn't even look up or wave, another reason to be angry. No one came to visit me while I was in hospital and I would sit and watch when other people called to see other patients.

I didn't know then that no one visited me because they wouldn't be able to leave me there and walk away. They had been told they could look through a window to see me so they knew I was all right but they were not to let me see them. I became insufferable, I felt no one loved or even liked me anymore!

I was still having eating problems so it became necessary to sort out some type of diet that would help me grow and stop all the probing and tests, just to help me lead an ordinary life. Hospital stays were not helping, in fact were doing the opposite. A sick child does not get better unless it feels someone cares about them, or, might even love them.

But the brighter side of that time was, I made a friend, a little girl who was a little older than me, who loved to sing and I loved to hear her singing so that little girl taught me the words of the first verse of a song which would be my favourite song forever!. 'The Wild Colonial Boy', which won me a prize at the Shelbourne Hotel Christmas Party that year, the reward was a hollow chocolate Father Christmas covered in silver paper with a picture of Father Christmas on it. That was me first and only party piece. If I could remember the second verse it would still be me best party piece!

The hotel had a Christmas party every year for the staff's children and there were hundreds of us. I thought it was great and I always had a great time, it was one of the signs of Christmas and the Hotel Christmas party was the conversation of the year for a long time before and a long time afterwards.

While I was too young to worry about what was going on anywhere except in me own small world the wider world was taking on it's own challenges. The War in Europe was coming to an end but the rationing went on.

....

Chapter 7

What The Papers Reported

The newspapers kept everyone up to date in the Donnelly household, a family never without a morning or evening paper. Me daddy never failed to come home from work in the morning without either The Press or The Independent newspaper folded in his outside jacket side pocket and at tea-time the Evening Press newspaper was delivered through the letterbox.

Here are some items of news reported in various papers for the year 1945.

1) Congratulations to Mr. Sean T. O'Kelly who was installed as the 2nd President of Ireland on 26 June

2) In the world of Medicine and Science it was the Discovery of Penicillin, by Sir Alex Fleming that made this year momentum.

3) The public was reminded that the New Gas Rationing Plan penalty for people exceeding the gas ration would be the disconnection of their supply. Not an empty threat!. At least it was the month of May and warmer weather was forecasted. People still had the choice of coal, or turf if the weather continued to be cold.

4) There was talk that the war was being won and better days ahead were predicted, but they also mentioned a crisis at Dublin Zoo due to a shortage of horse meat. The lions were beginning to feel decidedly hungry and were letting the visitors and the 'hands that fed them' know of their dilemma so some of the other smaller animals had to be killed to feed them.

5) Never a dull moment on the work front either. There was a dispute between the Federation Union of Employers and the discontented workforce of The Dublin Laundries. The workers refusing to do any more overtime when they were refused an extra week's holiday. They were already working very long hours.

6) Money of course was in very short supply to the many but for those working in high paying jobs in the Civil Service or were in business for themselves and there was always the possibility of a little money put aside, then this property that came on the market was a snip at the price. An attractive house on the seafront in Sandycove with 3 Reception rooms, 5 Bedrooms, 2 Lavatories, 2 Bathrooms and a Garage, a mere £5,000 and with furniture available on the 'Never, Never' at 'Cavendishes' of Grafton Street, well anything was possible!

7) Those who had the luxury of a car, were self-taught drivers driving around the streets of Ireland enjoying the freedom of the roads in the course of their business or pleasure were in for a surprise, shock, horror 'Driving Tests' for Motorists' likely! Times they were a changing, but, "THEY" didn't say when.

8) This fabulous advertisement must have put a smile on impoverished ladies faces when Abbey 'Sun Tan Lotion' for lovelier legs proclaimed their product to be, Sheerer than Silk without the expensive drawback of holes, ladders and tears. What a discovery! And what would the shareholders of Mulcahy's Bear Brand Stockings think about that?

9) And Finally : For Theatre goers the historical play 'Rossa' was showing to great audiences at the Abbey and the Opera 'La Traviata' opened it's season at the Olympia. It was also the year the Abbey Actor Cyril Cusack married Maureen Kiely and, and also a mention about the film 'This Woman in a Window' – a mental Jolt in Murder Mystery, showing at the Royal. 2 Oscars were awarded, one to Ingrid Bergman for her role in the film called 'Inn of the Sixth Happiness' and one to Barry Fitzgerald for his role in 'Going My Way'.

....

Chapter 8

Fairy Hill

After what seemed like a lifetime of Hospital stays, long and short, there was an agreement among the doctors and staff that there was little more they could do for me so I was moved to The Fairy Hill Open Air Hospital, in Baily, Co Dublin. Fairy Hill was opened in 1940 as a home for children forced to live away from Britain during the war.

After the war it was used as a convalescent home for children who needed care away from their home. I still wasn't putting on weight or eating all the things that were good for me even though there was great choice and, I was never forced to eat anything I didn't like, but they didn't see much improvement in me during my stay there either.

Fairyhill had been considered an oasis of goodness and there were lots of children like me there who needed building up and they all seemed happy and playful. There were no restrictions or treatments and everyone was given all sorts of lovely food to choose from, the nursing staff would play games, sing nursery rhymes, talk to us and help us join in but I was shy and I just waited with me eyes fixed to the door to see if someone I would recognize would come and take me away.

The days seem endless. I felt so lonely even though I was never alone. I wondered where me brothers and sisters were and what about me mammy and daddy, they didn't even visit. Was I ever going to see any of them again!

A month went by without a visit from anyone. I was told Fairy Hill was a long way from home and it wasn't easy to get to by bus for me mammy and daddy. When they did finally visit I was told later, that I refused to look at or acknowledge them so me daddy told the staff he wasn't leaving without me. I traveled back home to Clanbrassil Street in style by car, with me daddy, me mammy, and there was a baby in me mammy's arms which I tried to ignore. Me nose was rightly put out of place, things had been happening at home without me and I wasn't very happy about that. I wasn't the baby any more!

....

Chapter 9

Myra's arrival

Myra, me new sister had arrived when I wasn't looking. She was born four days after Germany surrendered and the War in Europe ended on 8 May 1945. It was a date in history the world would never forget and the celebrations and thanksgivings began in every city and country village all over the world.

There was great cheering and singing and dancing in the streets of Dublin as the news came over the wireless and the church bells of St. Patrick's Cathedral, Christchurch's Cathedral and the local Parish churches everywhere rang out to announce the good news and to invite everyone to celebrate and be together. People's doors were flung open and joy filled the air as everyone hugged and kissed, laughed and cried and thanked God that they were alive! I of course was oblivious to all this celebrating, but, I had survived!

Me diet included bananas, which were already scarce as with many other essentials, but the Donnelly children didn't worry too much about the lack of vegetables as long as there were potatoes. None of us were great lovers of vegetables.

There would be porridge for breakfast, with milk and a sprinkling of sugar on top to start the day. Potatoes was the stable diet and went with whatever meat or fish our mammy bought with peas or beans made up the meal for dinner. Mammy was good at making pies. but I don't remember much of that I was too young. Me mammy was a good cook I was told. I didn't seem to like anything that anyone might suggest would be good for me and help me grow, not even egg custard, rice or sago pudding, I can only admit to being a finicky child.

The only meat I would eat was mincemeat and that was every day. It seems everyone else made decisions about what I should eat but of course being a child I protested a lot. What I liked was not always what was given to me. Bread was kept to a minimum because me stomach protested when I was allowed to eat anything cooked that had flour in it and these included, bread, cakes and even biscuits but the doctors said I could eat Marietta biscuits as there wasn't a great deal of flour in them. To me brothers and sisters, Marietta biscuits became part of their diet also.

Chapter 10

Brian – Aileen - Scoil Bride

Myra, our newest addition, now nearly two years old, steady on her feet, chatting and smiling at everyone, was making her presence felt and was thriving. It was time for me to join Nuala at Scoil Bride.

I was following in the footsteps of me aunties Evelyn and Betty who had spent their early school years there. Aileen, Brian and Terry were already at Scoil Bride.

Me big brother Brian, born in August 1938 was showing promise as an artist though still young. His teachers discovered he had a natural flair and his drawings were always in perspective. He was also musical and began violin lessons when he was six years old. Years later he would take his rightful place at the Municipal School of Music and introduce us all to the joys of Classical Music, but his career would be in Commercial Art.

Aileen was now living part-time with Granny and our aunties Betty, Stella, Evelyn and our uncle Pearse since Terry was born. Granny seemed to think Aileen was being neglected by me mammy so she took Aileen to stay with them, she probably liked the idea of having a little one around the house again!. I believe it was quite common that the eldest grandchild went to live with their granny.

Aileen learnt to play the piano when she was tall enough to sit on the piano stool and could reach the foot pedals with her feet. She passed her 2nd Grade Honors Certificate at Munalap School of Music. Granny had a piano and very high hopes!.

Aileen, me big sister was born 1937 the year Douglas Hyde was inaugurated as President of Ireland. Aileen, the first twinkle to arrive, was born into the Donnelly household on the 8th May, the first grandchild and the eagerly awaited niece. She was a spring baby but too young to attend the Spring Show in Ballsbridge, Dublin 4. The month of May was a fashionable month in shops like Gleeson's in Camden Street where there was marvelous value in two-piece suits for day wear.

For formal occasions, there could be a visit to 'Arnott's' of Henry Street for that 'Crepe-de-Chine' dress matched by the 'Crepe-de-Chine' organdie coat at only £12.12s. To finish off the ensemble, a pair of Tyler's Bow Court shoes covered in suede. But Aileen was still in baby frocks and bootees, quite a few years away from the world of style and fashion! Little did anyone ever guess how Aileen would become a lady of style and a follower of fashion!

Chapter 11

Other News Items

Other Newspaper Items from 1937, the year Aileen turned a married couple into a family, and some from the year 1939,
(There were no new additions born into the family that year).

1) On 10 May The designer of the Hindeburg Zeppelin, Dr. Eckener died when 'IT' crashed at Lake Mooring Mast.

2) Aileen was but four days old on 12 May 1937 when the Coronation of King George VI and Queen Elizabeth took place The King was crowned King of Ireland and there were Protest Marches held in Dublin and in parts of Derry. The following day the Equestrian Bronze Statue of King George, which stood in Stephen's Green, Dublin, was blown up

3) On February 14th 1939 Pope Pius XI died at the age of 81 years. On March 2nd Eugenio Pacelli was elected as the next Pope taking the name Pope Pius XII. Eugenio Pacelli had been appointed Cardinal Secretary of State to Pope Pius XI. That same year W.B. Yeats died.

4) In 1939 Eamon DeValera announced that the Republic would remain neutral in the European war so when German bombs dropped on Carlow, Kildare, Louth , Meath, Wexford, Wicklow and the North Strand in Dublin, killing 34 people, with 9 injured and 300 houses destroyed or damaged it came as a shock to everyone. The German Government apologized and promised compensation. The other effect of the war was the shortage of paraffin oil.

5) On May 23, Mr. John D. Rockefeller the richest man in the world died of natural causes aged 85yrs.

6) On the brighter side of events, there was the annual gathering of 30,000 homing pigeons from England and Ireland at the Pigeon Derby in Kingsbridge – prize money of £1,600. On release, the pigeons took their bearings and headed for home, leaving some eggs behind!.

And last but not least:

7) For Theatre goers : There was Sandy Daw in 'The Means Test' on at the Olympia, George Clarke (Comedian) in 'George Ahoy' at the Gaiety and Helen Morgan in 'Karina' at the Theatre

■■

Mammy & Daddy at a Dress Dance

Some of us on a day out, Myra the youngest, then me, Nuala, Terry and Brian, with Aileen the eldest, in 1946.

Me younger brothers, Ciaran and Gerald
and youngest sister Rachel
looking very smart for Terry and Judy's Wedding in 1964.

Chapter 12

Uncle Pearse Marries Doris

On 8 May 1946 Pearse (me daddy's brother) married Doris Ervine in the Church of Our Lady of the Rosary on Harold's Cross Road. Pearse attended Synge Street Christian Brother's School until he passed his Leaving Certificate Exam. He then went to work for a Company called 'Auto Zero' in Blackpitts which was quite near to Granny's house. He was so close he was able to go home for his dinner to Granny's every day. He worked his way up to became the Manager. .

Doris worked as a Shorthand Typist in Conways of Wicklow Street before working for P.J.Kilmartins, Turf Accountants. Here's an account of how and where she met the love of her life Pearse.

Doris' life changed when she and her friend Maureen Gaynor decided to go to the Templeogue Tennis Club with their own boyfriends one evening but Doris said as soon as she saw Pearse, she thought he was the most handsome man in the room and at that moment there was no-one else for her. Pearse gave her a lift home on the crossbar of his bike.

They had a quiet Wedding.
....

Chapter 13

The Walk to School with Nuala

As I got stronger and reached me fourth birthday I walked with Nuala on the road to an Irish Education even if I did look too young and a bit small to be going to school! I think I was a quiet child and a loner but I can't be sure, but I liked the idea of new things happening and from what I was overhearing at home, school seemed to be something different. Myra and me were usually being put to bed when everyone else was taking out their school books to do their homework on the kitchen table and they could all read!.

Every week day Nuala and I walked from our house to school but sometimes Aileen would meet up with us and carry me, but I quickly learned the route we took. From Clanbrassil Street up Lombard Street West into Curzon Street towards Harrington Street past Harcourt Road and along the Adelaide Road to Earlsford Terrace and Scoil Bride which was tucked down a side turning.

Just before we reached the lane leading to the school we had to pass a Protestant Private ladies college. I couldn't see them as there was a high brown painted fence around their playground at the front of the school but I could hear them talking and laughing.

A couple of years after I had started school a neighbour from the grocer shop had gone on a Pilgrimage to Lourdes and had brought me back a Miraculous medal and chain which had been blessed. I was told not to show it off, but to keep it out of sight when I was passing that school or one of the girls might rush out and snatch it from me, 'They' don't like Catholic Medals, I was told!

I guarded the medal with me life and kept it out of sight with me arm across me buttoned up coat and a sharp eye on the school as I walked by with Nuala.

While I was at school the older girls wanted to mother mel and mother me they did when they decided to do me homework for me as well, even though there wasn't very much of that. Myra in later years remarked that I had only survived because I was jealous of her!

Nuala was born into the family during a very hot August in 1941 as the war raged across Europe. She became me carer and protector at school. It was at least a twenty minute walk to school and we called in to St. Kevin's Parish church on the way there and sometimes on the way back. Nuala got in trouble with mammy for being late home one afternoon. You see our daddy's bicycle had been stolen so Nuala took me with her, we called into St. Kevin's Church on Harrington Street and prayed for the safe return of daddy's bike. Nuala's prayers always seemed to be answered and when we got home that day daddy's bike had been found. Nuala was always 'Holy' so God always listened when she asked for favours!.

We made friends with a very nice lady who lived in one of the big houses near Dr. O'Leary house on the South Circular Road. The lady used to watch out for us either through her front window with the curtain pulled back, and she waved or she would stand at her front door. Sometimes on the way home she would invite us in for a chat, a glass of milk and a biscuit. I liked those times even though it was definitely a day when Nuala would be in trouble for being late home again!

I also learnt how to tell the time on the Roman Numeral Clock in McNally's Chemist shop window with the constant passing back and forth every day. I sometimes imagined I would have been able to find me own way to school there and back with me eyes closed.

I liked it at that school and became quite good at handwriting and spelling and loved the stories and rhymes, especially the rhyme 'Two Little Dickie Birds sitting on a wall.... I found it quite difficult to speak in Irish so I worried a lot but I did enjoy watching and listening to everyone else. It was a school where all the subjects and conversations were 'As Gaeilge'. If anyone was caught 'Ag Caint as Bearla' they were in trouble!. I soon began to understand "Cunas, dul a coladh agus na bi ag caint bearla" Nuala, who wasn't even two years older than me got a medal for her Irish speaking because she was so good, 'Maith an Cailín!.'

Despite liking Scoil Bríde there were times when I didn't want to be there and I would pretend I didn't feel well. Nuala would have to walk me back home. I don't ever remember hearing Nuala complain about me, but then again maybe she did! She couldn't have been that perfect, but Nuala did mind all the lessons she was missing.

One morning as we were hurrying to school I had a fall in Lombard street which left me with bleeding knees and a badly grazed hand with dirty grit in the cut and I couldn't or wouldn't stretch the palm of me hand or close it and I couldn't stop crying. I was threatened with having to see the doctor if I didn't let someone clean it. I let them!

....

Chapter 14

Enda arrives

During me first year at school, another new sister, born on March 26th 1947 was taking pride of place at home in the bottom drawer of the tallboy. She was baptized Enda but it would be many years before Enda would find out it was a name usually given to boys. It was only when she was asked to produce her birth certificate in order to apply for a place to take The Intermediate Exam that she found the Births Registrar had her down as a male child!

When Enda was a few months old our mammy noticed that something was not quite right about Enda, who didn't seem to be moving one leg as much as the other so she asked Aileen to bring Enda up to see what Granny had to say. After the visit mammy asked if granny had noticed anything and Aileen told mammy that granny said she should bring Enda to the hospital to see what the doctors would say.

The terrible news was Enda had contracted Infantile Paralysis (Polio) and was rushed to The Fever Hospital in Cork Street immediately. Enda had been very unfortunate to be affected by Polio before a Vaccine had been discovered. The long awaited Vaccine was discovered by Dr. Jonas Salk in April 1955.

The long wait began as to how Polio would affect Enda and if anyone else in the family had been in contact with the disease. As Polio was contagious all us children were tested and found to be clear but at that time children were still not allowed to visit people in hospital, even if the patient was family. Poor Enda was to spend a long time in hospital.

Over the following couple of years whenever Enda was to be discharged from hospital she seemed to develop some kind of infection which delayed her coming home. So time went by and because of the restriction of children visiting, she was out of sight and out of mind to those closer to her in age but not to Aileen, Brian, Terry and Nuala.

The outcome of the diagnosis was, the muscles in one of Enda's legs were wasted and would not grow to normal size, she would need a caliper to help her walk after her treatment in hospital was completed. Enda was to have many stays in the Orthopaedic Hospital in Clontarf for many years. These hospital stays would mostly be during the long summer school holiday months for the operations she would endure. Meself and Myra and those who were younger than Enda were not really aware how serious Polio could affect people.

....

Chapter 15

Myra's Battles with Mammy,
Myra's Walk Of Fame Under a Horse

Nuala and me became a trio when we were joined by Myra when she was old enough and ready to make the walk to school. Myra had a big smile and she was a great hit with the girls and teachers of Scoil Bríde and she loved going to school.

At home she had daily battles with our mammy. Myra wasn't very good at taking 'No' for an answer and was very stubborn and would stand her ground. She blankly decided she wasn't eating porridge, that it made her sick so she ranted and raged, cried and carried on refusing to eat it until our mammy eventually gave in to her and she was given Cornflakes!

It was unheard of that mammy would give in to anyone. Myra was not liked by those who had to continue eating porridge or starve, but our mammy wouldn't listen to them. Why only 'Her', why couldn't 'Everyone' have cornflakes?' was the constant moan but wasn't dared said out loud or in mammy's hearing when they saw Myra eating cornflakes, it wasn't fair!

Where the house was situated on the main road there was the constant worry that if the front door was left open any one of us could walk out on to the road, get knocked down or possibly killed. That nightmare almost became a reality when Myra walked straight under a horse (possibly the coalman's horse) no-one knew or cared whose horse it was, or what colour it's coat was, or how big or small it was, or had it had new shoes shod recently or was it overworked? Except that Myra had walked under a horse on one of the busiest main roads in Dublin and managed to get to the other side of the road without being killed!

It was as though time stopped for those who saw it happening and froze on the spot. It didn't bear thinking about, what if she had been a fraction of an inch taller or her hair ribbon had tickled the horse's belly?

••

Chapter 16

Ciaran Born and The Death of Uncle Frank

After four girls in a row, in 1948 Ciaran a brother, another May baby joined the family, then there were eight of us, five girls and three boys. It seemed May was a good month to be born because as well as Ciaran, Myra and Aileen being born in that month, me daddy's and Auntie Stella's birthdays were in May also so there was great reason to celebrate but an expensive month as well.

We still lived in the same house on the same street and there we were to remain through our growing up years. Sadly Uncle Frank died. He was greatly missed by us all. For him to have stayed that long in our house where another baby made its entrance every couple of years, well, he really must have loved us and felt loved in return. Everyone mourned the loss of uncle Frank when all his personal things were removed from his room upstairs.

Because the family was getting bigger and the recent addition being a another boy it was decided the back bedroom would now be the boys' bedroom, and the front remained the girls bedroom which had two double beds, one single bed and a cot in the corner. Each room had a tallboy and a wardrobe and the girl's room had a dressing table. There were two large windows in the girl's bedroom which overlooked the main road at the front of the house and the boy's bedroom had a back window overlooking the back yard and they could see the backs of all the houses down Clanbrassil Terrace and into Mulcahy's Factory car-park.

We girls shared the front bedroom with our mammy. Our daddy slept there when he had nights off. Our daddy worked as a night Hotel Porter in a hotel so we didn't see much of him at night-time. Daddy slept during the day. He arrived home after everyone had left for school and he was only around when we were having our tea in the evening. He had two nights off every two weeks when he and mammy would dress up and go out to the pictures, visit friends or go dancing. They looked lovely. We would be asleep by the time they came back.

The boys slept in the back bedroom and as Brian and Terry were members of The Pro Cathedral Church choir in Marlborough Street they could be heard practicing their singing in the early hours of the mornings

especially at the weekends.
    Everyone was an early riser. We always thought that mammy liked the boys more. She never asked the boys to take the baby with them when they were going out. Brian was her favourite and everyone else was a little bit jealous.

Chapter 17

Home life – Illness – Fine-combs and Flack

Home life was mostly spent living in the kitchen, the warmest room in the house but if more than one of us was ill with anything contagious such as chicken pox, measles or even the usual coughs, colds or fevers, the girls' bedroom, which was normally freezing most of the year round, would be turned in to a cozy sick room with a big fire roaring in the open grate and smoke whirling up the chimney, if we were lucky!

We would have our meals together and get better quicker, save on mammy's feet running up and down the cold linoleum covered stairs.

From what I heard or possibly remembered was that Nuala and Terry had their tonsils removed at the same time in the Meath Hospital at the bottom of Long Lane. Whooping cough, TB, polio and ringworm to name a few were some of the contagious diseases going around at the time so being a large family these diseases would not have escaped us. Sometimes it was difficult to know if the cough was whooping cough or not as the sound was horrendous to listen too.

We also had our share of nits and head-lice, they came, made the rounds from child to child all around the school and back to all our lovely shiny heads of hair. The dreaded steel fine comb was dragged through our hair and the smell of flack attacked our nostrils through the night.

Fleas where another bane of me mammy's life and ours as well. No matter what was done they came. Great dustings of DDT was sprinkled in the bedrooms between the blankets and in the pillows and anywhere mammy thought flees might be hiding. They were attacked and they went, but they came back again and again.

Every family around could always count on their company! One of the most awful, unsightly and revolting items that hung from the ceiling in our house was, the fly-paper strip. It would have been just hung minutes before the invaders got stuck fast. What could have been the attraction?

Chapter 18

Gerald's Arrival – The Marion Year

Gerald, a blond, blue-eyed baby boy was born February 1950 bringing the family total to nine children in our two bedroom house.

1950 was the beginning of The Marion Year and the year George Bernard Shaw, the great play-writer died. It was the year of the Pageant of St. Patrick which was performed in Croke Park Stadium.

Those of us who could walk, walked the route with thousands of like-minded people to watch a very spectacular and historic event taking place on a grand scale in the open air. With splendid lightings, sound effects, costumes with hundreds of people taking part. It was amazing. There was a wonderful atmosphere and it was a great achievement in bringing so many people together. We walked together as a family.

It was the year I was being prepared to received me First Holy Communion - a very important day in the life of every catholic child. But before we received our First Communion we all had to make our First Confession. Now at this time I did not give a thought to anyone else's well being. I behaved like any other child, the world spun round just for me. Never mind what those at the hospital were saying, I lived on bread and Blue Band® margarine, foil wrapped for freshness 2/4d a lb. 'It costs a bit more but it's worth it!' That was the slogan, but it just didn't taste the same as butter, no matter who said it did!. Everyone could tell the difference between Blue Band and Butter? Couldn't they? Of course they could!

The idea that the family had been brought up on Blue Band could have been the downfall of a happy romance when on a future occasion when a member of the family had been proposed to and the mother of the future bridegroom found out that her son might have to eat Blue Band Marge and not Irish Butter, God Forbid! She might really have opposed the Marriage as the future bride may not be good enough for her son. Now, why wasn't someone listening?

The marriage went ahead and they BOTH ate butter. Was there a happy ending? Did it matter whether they eat Marge or Butter? We'll see....

Every day I would only eat mince meat and potatoes, even on Fridays (which were days of abstinence from meat) and that was unheard of in a good catholic family to even have meat in the house never mind being cooked and eaten. It was usually fish on Fridays and not many of the family were very keen on fish so Fridays were days of moans and groans, 'I don't like fish' but it was that or go hungry. But as my First Confession was looming ahead me mammy reminded me nearly every time she caught sight of me, usually when she was in bad form, which seemed to be most of the time! "Don't forget to tell the priest, you eat meat on Fridays!".

....

Chapter 19

First Confession and First Communion Preparation

I don't know how many there were in the class but we were paraded through the streets from Adelaide Road to the University Church, St. Stephen's Green. The church was small, very dark and very quiet, that was until we shuffled and pushed our way none too quietly through its doors. We had all been told what to expect in the confessional but the reality was much more frightening. Outside the Confessional we all knelt close together as though the church mightn't hold us all. We made four rows, two on each side of the priest's box.

When it was my turn I found myself in a little box-like room, which I could just about turn around in, but I didn't dare. There was a kneeler, but it wasn't very high, a crucifix and pitch darkness. I knelt and waited, thinking of all the things I was supposed to say and trying not to forget the words.

After what seemed like forever I heard a jingle of curtain rings and a voice. As I couldn't see anything I thought it must be GOD. I started off in parrot fashion as I had learnt ' Bless me Father for I have sinned ...'

I prattled off a list I had memorized which I thought must be me sins, in a not too quiet whisper, forgetting of course 'the eating of minced-meat on Fridays!' After I'd finished, 'GOD' mumbled a few words. I was told to say one Hail Mary. I stumbled through the 'O me God... ' In a daze I found meself back with me class waiting to take the walk back to school in an orderly line.

My First Holy Communion preparation was in the form of having a piece of blotting paper which represented the Host being placed on me tongue. So there we were a whole class of children aged around six to seven years old, standing with hands joined together, fingers pointing upwards, and thumbs crossed, eyes closed with our mouths open waiting to receive a piece of blotting paper in the shape of a Holy Communion wafer practicing for that very special day.

We all had to keep our eyes closed so by the time the teacher got to me, me mouth was all dry, me tongue had been in the air too long, the blotting paper got stuck to the roof of me mouth, and I remember not being allowed to dislodge it with me teeth!. Being nearly seven years old was a very impressionable age.

May, Our Lady's month was a month when children all over Dublin received their First Holy Communion and it was a beautiful, sunny day as all May days seemed to be then. I was excited inside.

For one whole day out of 365 days, because it wasn't a Leap Year, I was special, important, in me white dress and veil, hand knitted knee socks which me mammy knitted, white shoes, and gloves which were probably knitted by me mammy as well, if I did have gloves?. Everyone told me I looked like an angel but I knew that anyway. I felt like I thought an angel would feel.

I had to meet me class at the church at 8.30am for Mass and to receive me First Holy Communion. Not much attention was paid to Mass by us, but as to how we looked in our new clothes and me mind was distracted thinking about important things like, who would I be brought to visit first, like how much money I would get and of course what to spend it on.

When Mass was ended we had to stay together and return to school for the class photograph. For the rest of the day I was brought to visit me granny and me aunties. Auntie Stella had a camera so she took a photo of me standing at the gap in the hedge in their front garden. Then to visit friends and neighbours, just to keep up tradition and to boost me Communion money. I felt wonderful. I liked it when people admired me on the street and were amazed that I was nearly seven years old. I looked the size of a three year old.

As a special treat on me Communion Day when all the visiting was over Nuala, Myra and me went to Delaney's shop in Clanbrassil Street to buy a box of Chivers Jelly. We managed to chew it square by square with difficulty before reaching home, all because we were always being told not to eat raw jelly squares. We never could remember why. It was like the forbidden fruit. No one would ask why, maybe because that might have been the give-a-way that we had eaten some. Jelly cubes were only for making into 'Afters' by pouring boiling water over them, stirring until the cubes melted and then left on the window sill in the yard until it set and became a bowl of edible jelly. Sadly, wonderful days come to an end and that day did with high-tea of special creamy butterfly cakes and jam sponges, homemade by our mammy, with everyone sitting together and that's what made it special.

....

Chapter 20

News

Newspaper items for 1952

1) The annual May Processions started at Mt Argos, The Passionist Priests Church near Harold's Cross, with the Artane Boy's band, the United City Confraternity, pupils from St. Clare's School, Harold's Cross, the Mt. Argos Catholic Boy Scouts, children from the surrounding neighbourhoods and of course the 'Donnelly sisters' Nuala, Myra and me.

2) There was some trouble in CIE as an appeal was sent to the workers to end their strike. 1,000 men were involved and goods trains to Bray and the Boat trains to Dun Laoghaire were affected. It had even spread to the Grand Canal Depot which operated these trains. Trains would stop at various stations and then return to the depot causing a lot of disruption. Other means of transport were used to send Cattle Exhibits to the Spring Show from neighbouring towns and CIE lorries took away loads of cattle and sheep from Midland Towns.
    The Department. of Posts & Telegraphs made arrangements for the collection and distribution of letter mails to those places affected but a temporary suspension was placed on the accepting of any other post. Airmail post arriving at Shannon Airport was then being flown to Dublin by Aer Lingus. After a lot of disruption and negotiation the Rail Strike ended on May 5th.

3) Corus Iompar Eireann (CIE) started an advertising campaign to encourage people to
'See Ireland By Bus' with offers of 'Day Trips from Dublin by Touring bus – See Ireland with   CIE :Glendalough & Avoca 10/-,
Liffey Valley & Blessington Lakes 10/-
Sightseeing in Dublin City 6/-
Coastal & Mountain Tour 4/-

4) Was it Luck or did 'Our Lady' intervene when the C.I.E. Strike miraculously ended just as the Pilgrimage Season opened on May 8th the Month of Our Lady?. Special trains brought pilgrims and invalids from St. Mary's Hospital, Rialto to the Grotto of Our Lady of Knock.

5) It was also time for the Annual Visit to the Shrine of Blessed Oliver Plunket when 4,000 pilgrims went by train and bus to Drogheda to pray for his Canonization.

6) The first Mobile Unit for the National Blood Transfusion Association was formally opened by Mrs O'Kelly, The President's wife and she thanked the 160 staff of Aer Lingus who had given about twenty gallons of blood.

During her speech Mrs. O'Kelly appealed to women in particular to help make it fashionable to be a Blood Donor by saying 'They had time during the day. They were seen as the all caring people who were in touch with the suffering of others, they understood the fragility of human life and the danger of death. They understood about people's needs and had the care of children in their hearts.'

7) It was also the year Orangemen said 'NO' to Unity or Communism – which was proposed and passed at the Orange gathering at Finaghy on 12 July.

8) And a woman from Gortahurk was fined £2 at Derrylin County Court for having been in possession of a half pint of Poteen which was found in the thatch roof of her cottage. She denied any knowledge of it!

9) And some breaking news from America that might be of some interest to someone, somewhere, was that their great statue of Liberty which didn't often hit the headlines of the Irish papers but today it was because it's Liberty's light was snuffed out, the first time ever in recorded history, even during the war it had glowed over the Harbour of New York The cause was thought to be of an electrical cable fault! It was felt the world should know about this!

10) At last some good news for Irish speaking families. Under the auspices of Clann na hEireann, in Parnell Square, Dublin, there was an offer of two weeks holidays at the small cost of only £2. The holiday would be spent playing games, (indoor & outdoors), there would be picnics and singsongs. All the enjoyment would be through

the Irish Language. A great time was being offered for all!

12) There was a day of great excitement at Mulcahy's Factory right next door to our house. When Mr Morrissey, the Minister for Industry opened the £100,000 extension to the factory of Messrs Mulcahy Bros. Hosiery Manufacturers at 99 Lr. Clanbrassil Street. He urged the workers to become members of his or her Trade Union and if each and everyone of the workers adhered to those principles they would have fewer disturbances in industry. He said the new extension would bring them nearer to producing the 30,000 pairs of ladies stockings which passed over the drapers counters each day and as soon as that was achieved he would recommend to the Government to reduce imports drastically.

12) There was great uproar in the Dail as to the Query with regards The Opening of Letters in the Post Office.
The Question put to the Minister for Posts & Telegraph was, 'In what circumstances and by whose Authority was it alright for private letters while in course of post, be removed and handed over to State Officials, to open, read and re-seal before delivery to addresses and, how many people were effected?.'
The Reply was: That in accordance with Sections 56 of Post Office Act of 1908, a warrant issued by the Minister for Justice stated that it would not be in the public's interest to know the number of persons being examined under this order.

13) Decisions were being talked about raising the School Leaving age to 15 but the decision was postponed until April 1953 due to difficulties in providing school accommodation and qualified teachers, many 14 year olds breathed a sigh of relief and looked forward to getting a job and having some money in their pockets.

14) Tougher penalties for people were brought in with regard to those not paying their Income Tax. The threat was that their salary or wage would be taken from them, and also the possibility of their worldly goods being sold and possible imprisonment.

15) Good news for Post Office Staff: The postal staff requested a 40 hour 5 day week and it was agreed at their Annual Conference in Limerick. Also agreed a monetary allowance to all those whose duties exceeded 10 hours covering period. A six day delivery to all rural areas and the closing of all public counters at 6pm.

16) *And Finally - The Latest Must Haves for Ladies: Get into shape!. Not an advertisement for a run around the block or a good healthy walk around Blackrock but a 'must visit' Invitation to Cassidy's, the draper shop in Georges Street for their latest Sale of Ladies Corsets with popular side hooking styles also a black lacing corset with strong front–lacing for that near perfect figure, for all fashion conscious women.*

Chapter 21

Newspapers and their Uses

As I mentioned before, our house was never without a newspaper and it was one of the most essential commodities of our time. A house was not a home without a newspaper.

The Independent and the Evening Press covered all the main events and if you were anyone important, had done something special, or were seen with the right people you just might see a photograph of yourself in it! We were delighted to see a photograph of our daddy standing in the background, behind Elizabeth Taylor when she was staying at the Gresham Hotel where he worked. He also managed to get her Autograph.

The Newspaper, apart from keeping everyone up to date on Politics and Religion, and who was doing what and where (it is doubtful the subject of sex was mentioned anywhere, (not in front of us children anyway!). Of course the results of the horse racing at the Curragh and Lepardstown and the dog racing in Harold's Cross was very important and then there were the results of the Gaelic football matches in Croke Park and Landsdown Road, they got a mention also on the sports page.

There was the children's page and weekly painting competition at which I painstakingly coloured in the picture with me favourite colours from me paint box of eight colours, with great concentration, not every week but often enough, waited for the paint to dry and sent it away having filled out the entry form in me best handwriting. Me mammy would always say 'Write small, Deirdre' but there was never enough room on the line for all the letters in me name!

The most important question to me was, who had won the painting competition? Surprise! 'They' (the judges) didn't recognise my extraordinary talent, so no appearance of me name anywhere!.

During the wet, cold, damp, winter months me daddy would wrap some newspaper around his feet and ankles inside his socks to keep his feet warm while he was at work. His job involved a lot of walking and standing around especially during the night shift. Brown paper did a better job of keeping the cold out but it was a lot scarcer to get.

Newspaper served as toilet paper also. It was cut up into neat squares, threaded on a string and hung on a nail (nothing fancy!) in the toilet. Other uses, shining up the black fire-range, for standing shoes on when they were polished, for protecting the kitchen table when the tin bath was being used, and, for wrapping up the single of chips to stop our hands from getting burnt, the chips wouldn't have tasted so good if they hadn't been wrapped in newspaper!

It seemed very appropriate when a job appeared in the Irish Independent paper 'There's Money in Waste Paper' was the important catchphrase to catch the eye. Men of good standing, with suitable premises to act as buying agents for the National Waste Paper Co. Waterford. Apply now!

••

Chapter 22

How to Lay The Perfect Fire

The kitchen range was lit every morning for cooking meals and boiling water for cleaning, laundry and the Saturday night baths but mainly for keeping the house warm, as it could feel very damp at times.

The grate was raked out every morning and hand twisted knots of paper, a few sticks of wood from the bundles that were bought in 'Mr. Somer's Shop' across the road laid on top. The cinders left over from the previous evening were used and sometimes a firelighter or two that smelt of paraffin was needed, before the fire was lit and fed with fresh coal to give the house the smell of a lived in home.

The coal was delivered on a cart pulled by a dray horse wearing really big cloppety, clop shoes. The coalman heaved the sacks over his shoulder and was bent over with the weight. It was hard to see the coalman's face as he was always as black as the coal he carried. He had to carry it through the hall, down the passage and empty the sack into the scullery space under the stairs, coal dust billowing overhead and settling on everything around.

Sometimes turf or briquettes were used and when it was really cold a 'Blue Flame 'Alladin' Oil Heater' was lit as well. As with a lot of items, if they are not treated well, they retaliate in their own unique way. With this, much treasured, piece of mobile heating it variably needed regular care and attention to keep it up and working and family friendly. It was the management of the wick, which, when not cleaned properly would issue forth black spiraling smoke, Cough, Cough. But we could always tell of a job well done when a blue flame flickered behind its Perspex window.

....

Chapter 23

Back Yard – Cats, Rats and the Mice came too!

We were such a large family and with clothes that had to be washed and dried as we had so few, as well as sheets and maybe a blanket or two, we were lucky to be the proud possessors of a yard.

Our scenic view from the window from the kitchen was a view to behold. Clothes hanging on two lines and our very own evergreen bush which attracted a few birds that the boys could hear singing in the early mornings, but the sound I heard most was the cry of the sea gulls. They seemed to be everywhere whirling constantly round and round the flag-pole on Mulcahy's Factory Building and looking like giants and threatening with wide spanning wings and big beaks but it was a sound I loved. Their flying display was supposed to be a sign of rain or stormy weather on the way. A prediction that could have meant rain every day, but it didn't.

The yard was surrounded by a wall for privacy. Behind that wall was a small space and then another wall separating the garden from Mulcahy's car park. I was never brave enough to climb that wall so it kept its secrets, if it had any, from me.

The yard was a perfect place for the mice and rats to run in and out and scurry about, and they were very cheeky!. I was not afraid of the rats or mice as long as I could only see them and there was a window or door between them and me.

We always had a family cat or two or sometimes even as many as a dozen kittens depending on how big a litter our two female cats produced. The family could instinctively tell when a new litter was due. Someone would find our heavily pregnant cat hiding in one of the wardrobes and it would begin scratching just as we were falling asleep, leaving us to think there were mice in the bedroom ready to bite at our toes or fingers. I never slept with me leg or arm hanging over the bed, just in case!

Then one cat would try to move into the other female cat's bed and when she was frightened off she would be found in the coal-hold under the stairs where she would safely deliver her litter. Me daddy was getting so fed up with all these new kittens, he drowned one but it was an experience he would never repeat.

There were so many cats sometimes it was hard to find an empty chair to sit on. Me daddy would even give his chair to a cat rather than disturb it, and say 'This chair is not big enough for both of us, I better move!' and he would ask one of us for a chair. The question was, 'As there were so many cats around, why did we have rats and mice?'

There was one beautiful black cat that Nuala brought home from the cat and dog's home. The cat was a great mouse catcher. Nuala was told 'the cat' used to work for Brown Thomas's in Grafton Street!. It couldn't have come with a finer reference, she got the job!.

We did play ball games in the yard remembering to miss the kitchen window, sometimes one or two of us took a chair out and sat in the sun to read a book.

Chapter 24

Enda - Home from Hospital

As with lots of big families, one more addition never seems to make much difference so when mammy surprised us by asking 'How would you like another sister?' We thought that was great news and Enda was finally brought back home from the hospital.

Enda was not a baby but a little girl with lovely dark brown hair and a look of surprise on her face with all our strange faces looking at her. She wouldn't have remembered us from when she was a baby.

Our sister Enda now wore a caliper on her bad leg which was very thin because polio had stopped her leg muscles from developing. She needed that support to help her walk, but she also had to wear a lighter caliper at night. She was given the cot to sleep in. We were fascinated by her for some time and were even very considerate and nice to her.

As time passed we became less fascinated by her when we noticed all she had to do was swing her leg with the caliper and she could kick like a mule and we would be left with a bruise but nothing more serious. No one could get close enough to retaliate. This was just too much to take so we decided it was nicer to have Enda as a friend. Enda was back to stay.

As Enda approached school age the grown-ups agreed that she would not be able to walk the distance to Scoil Bríde. There was no talk of us taking a bus, as though no one thought about such means of travel and there were buses but there was definitely no special school bus laid on for those less able to walk.

You might suppose that there was no money for such luxuries but in actual fact no buses went down Adelaide Road. Buses traveling along the South Circular Road turned into Camden Street on the route to town and those coming from Rathgar or Rathmines went down Harcourt Street. Anyway, it was decided, we, Nuala, Myra and me would transfer to Scoil Náisiúnta, Warrenmount in Blackpits, which was about three to five minutes away from where we lived if we ran. It was also time for Aileen to change schools and she transferred to Terenure. That was the end of the line for the Donnelly family attending Scoil Bríde.

....

Chapter 25

Regrets on Leaving Scoil Bride

Aileen had attended Warrenmount school for a very short period but she was not happy. She had no regrets, Aileen was left handed and there wasn't the understanding about being left-handed so when she was being forced to use her right hand which she couldn't, a change of school was decided on.

This would be the first experience for the rest of us being taught by nuns. It was the teaching Order of the Presentation Sisters. The Low Babies and High Babies classes were taught by lay teachers, but the teaching staff for the rest of the school were the Sisters, though for various other curricular activities there were lay teachers. The head nun always looked quite cross and fearsome to me. Scoil Bride had only lay teachers.

So, no more walks along the South Circular Road. No more visiting that nice lady who would give us a biscuit on our way back from school. No more dropping into St Kevin's Church for special favours on the way there and back and I would miss the big Roman Clock in McNally's chemist shop window. I had liked that walk very much holding on to Nuala's hand and liked being carried to school by Aileen when I was younger. There wouldn't be anyone else from the family following in our footsteps to Scoil Bride.

Brian and Terry had already moved on to Coláiste Mhuire in Parnel Square to attend secondary school. It was there the multi-talented Brian took up Irish dancing and took part in the concerts held in the school hall. Brian was on stage wearing the traditional Irish dancing costume worn by male dancers, sporting a green jacket, a kilt of orange Irish Tweed with matching shoulder shawl held on with a Tara brooch, he was part of a set of dancers. He looked smashing and everyone was proud of him.

Brian joined the Legion of Mary and one of his jobs was to collect the kids from around the neighbourhoods in the city and bring them to the children's Mass in the Pro Cathedral Marlborough Street and leave them there. Then he and Terry would go back to sing in the Pro-Cathedral choir for the 12 o'clock Mass.

With Terry being in the scouts and Brian in the Legion of Mary they were often called on or would 'offer' to do some good deeds and maybe that was what brought Brian to granny's house on a nice bright sunny day.

Granny was the proud owner of a garden at the back and in the front of her house. The front garden was grass and had a hedge all round it. The back garden had grass, some flowers, a small hedge and a big lilac bush that flourished. Brian arrived to do some digging in the garden and cut back that wonderful smelling lilac bush that was laden with purple flowers reaching to the sky and overhanging into Mrs. Hopper's garden right at the fence where granny and Mrs. Hopper used to gossip (or was it just chatting they were engrossed in?)

There was Brian with the gardening pick, held high, ready to make its mark on granny's garden, he missed and put the pick straight into the middle of his foot. There were screams, blood and panic everywhere and Brian's foot attached to the pick. Michael Ball, Evelyn's future husband to the rescue, lifted Brian onto his bicycle crossbar and away to Meath Street Hospital they rode.

....

Chapter 26

Starting Warrenmount – Friends down the Lane

Warrenmount School was just around the corner down Clanbrassil Terrace, (which was called The Lane) and this was where all, or nearly all our friends lived. On the left side of the Lane, at Number 5 lived Margaret and Jimmy (who had a crush on me and used to buy me slides and ribbons). Ann lived at Number 6. Betty, Thomas, Paddy and John (a surprise brother when Betty was 16 years old and in secondary school) at Number 7. At Number 8 there was Joey, Sheila, Maura (my friend) Charlie, Noeleen, Angela and Thomas. They later moved into Number 3. Marie and Pauline who were adults and their brother Tim lived at Number 9. Marie and her mammy played a big part in all our lives. Finally at number 10 lived Phyllis, Roseline and Liam.

    We had our fights and disagreements just like other normal kids on the street: It was never 'Turn the other cheek." If someone hit one of us, we hit back, and it was one for all and all for one if outsiders tried to push in.

    On the opposite side of the Lane there were cottages where Tony Jackson lived and next door to Tony was Maisie Ellis who lived in her two roomed cottage with a yard at the back where she kept pigs and chickens and collected slops to feed them. Her front door was cut in two. The half door to her house was kept open most of the time. She liked us 'Donnellys' and if anyone said anything against us, she would say 'You watch now, those Donnellys will do well for themselves'. She was really our best friend and everyone needed a friend like Maisie.

    Then past Faddle Alley there were a few more cottages, (These were demolished later, all the families who were living there were re-housed.) A very quick walk on the opposite side led us to the slaughter house where horses were shot and the smell followed us wherever we went, and the horses' blood flowed in the gutter. Then across Blackpitts to our new home of education where the nuns were going to perform miracles with us, the new intake of Donnelly children.

    The school was also close to tenement houses close by but none of our family were allowed to play with or be associated with the children who lived in those sort of houses but like all curious children we used to stare at the twin sisters who wore wide rimmed funny hats that covered their whole heads and seemed to balance on their ears. People whispered that they didn't have any hair, that they were bald! We would wait in hope that their hats might fall off or be blown off by a strong wind so we could see for our selves. They were adult twins who suffered from alopecia, but we didn't know that then.

Nuala was clever and hardworking and got a place in fifth class. When I was tested by the head nun she decided I would benefit by staying back one more year. Myra and Enda went into lower classes, so none of us would be in the same class.

The best years of me life were not spent at school. I still wasn't keen on any type of school or place where I would have to sit for hours and do some work, that wasn't me idea of fun, so Warrenmount School wasn't in the 'like' section either. I was petrified of the nuns and forever anxious, but I very soon realised that it was better to learn than not to learn. The consequences of not learning was to be slapped with a strap or a cane on the hand, whichever was handiest to reach at that moment.

I was as cunning as the next and learnt to copy everything from the girl next to me. I was put beside a girl named Maura Smith who was friend from the Lane. Maura was tall with dark curly hair and always had a ribbon in her hair. She had very deep set brown eyes and a very pale complexion. She was also seen as a delicate child.

It wasn't long before the Sister realised I was copying so I was moved beside Betty Gorman, another friend from the Lane. As I was still relatively new even Betty was obliging, so in six months I achieved exactly NOTHING. But, finally the giveaway was, I had the right answer to a sum and half the sum missing, that warranted another move in the class.

I was put beside Noeleen Urell who lived in Kevin Street but we didn't know each other. Noeleen was about one inch taller than me but always neat and tidy. We got on very well together and we liked each other. We swapped everything we had but when it came to arithmetic I was stuck. After about ten minutes of looking and waiting, I said to Noeleen, 'Well, come on!' and Noeleen's reply was 'I'm waiting for you!' 'I don't know sums' I whispered and she just groaned. We sat and doodled for the rest of the lesson and worried about what might happen to us because neither of us had managed to copy or put any answers to the sums. Sister just looked at the copy-books and walked away. Me and Noeleen were left together. With a great deal of patience, effort, and understanding the Sister taught us arithmetic and I liked it very much. It was really worth the effort and I never looked back.

As we settled into our new school we were introduced to 'The Black Babies' and quickly caught on to the expression, 'A Penny for the Black Babies'. Every child in the school was given a blue card with the print of a rosary on it. For every penny we gave, 2 holes were pierced into the card with a pin and when all the beads had been pierced and the rosary was complete and signed by the teacher we were allowed to give the black baby a name.

....

Chapter 27

Me Mammy

Now me mammy was not a mammy with patience. The expression 'She had so many Children she didn't know what to do!' would possibly describe her. She always seemed to be cross. I was never aware of her being happy. She didn't have great patience. She didn't gush at us if we did something good or exciting.. She wasn't fond of us being around the house either.

Mammy was a believer in fresh air being good for us. When we were not in school we were on the street from early morning, especially during the school holidays and at weekends. It didn't matter if it was winter or whether we liked it or not. Maybe she just couldn't stand the noise of so many children around the house. It seemed that everyone else down the Lane was allowed to stay in bed half the day.

Myra and me used to sit on one particular doorstep or on the low wall beside one particular friend's house with our backs leaning against the railings, a terrible nuisance to her mammy. Even when she told us to sit somewhere else we didn't bother to move, we didn't have anywhere else to go.

We somehow got the feeling she wasn't very glad to see us Every time we knocked on her door or shouted, 'Is … coming out to play?' through her letterbox, no one would open the door to our letterbox rattling. She never invited us in even if it was raining, snowing, or just plain freezing cold. We didn't bother too often going back home either as it was only on the rare occasions we were allowed back into our house during the day except at mealtimes.

On a bitterly cold day I decided I definitely wasn't going out so when no one was looking I perched myself on the gas meter situated close by the hall-stand where the winter coats were warm and provided protective cover and their linings began to warm me up as my body-heat clung to them. I desperately wanted to let sleep take over but as I sat there on me hunkers on the cold metal of the meter, squashed for space, I found it was not the most comfortable place to find sleep. Me mind remained alert to all the sounds of the nearly empty house.

Even indoors it felt cold, so outside must have been a lot worse.

The house being on the main road, I could hear the traffic as it trundled by and it seemed to block out any movement that might be happening in the kitchen … I knew there was someone … in the kitchen … me mammy … who just wouldn't understand.

I sat, not daring to move even by shifting position in case me foot slipped to the linoleum floor or made a noise. Me body was beginning to ache in the cramped space and I began to feel quite numb all over. I had no idea what me mammy was doing as I couldn't hear a sound, except me own heart beat.

The sound of coal-carts and horses, voices and milk deliveries and even the dust from the street seemed to seep through the letter-box. I could hear the buses going up and down, people calling to each other and the silence of the house all round me. There were no letters delivered that morning so there wasn't any need for me mammy to come into the hall.

The ticking of the meter clock reminded me of how long a minute felt. Was it worth the fear of being caught? I asked meself. Logic said, ' NO!' but too late now. I decided I might as well go out, only to find the door lock was too high for me to reach, so there was nothing I could do but sit tight until some one came back.

....

Chapter 28

Swallowed Tooth

As I was fitting in with school I was down for a medical checkup and blood tests and it was decided I might as well see a dentist and have me teeth checked as well.

I was about seven years old and I'd had bad experiences with the dentist in The Carnagie Building, Lord Edward Street where they wanted to take out me bad tooth without gas - can you believe that? I refused to open me mouth and just sat and cried through clenched teeth until I was brought home by mammy who wasn't short in letting me know how angry she was!.

I had also been previously brought to the school dentist in Cornmarket Dental Health Centre and I wasn't happy with them either (and visa versa.) Anything to do with doctors or mention of injections and I became a mad child. I was eventually brought to the dentist at Harcourt Street hospital who agreed to use gas.

Me mammy brought me and I was admitted early in the morning and I didn't remember being put to sleep, but I could smell the gas as I inhaled and I remembered the nightmares that went with it, those never ending spirals of colours weaving in and out of vision and weird sounds and words 'ether, ether' going round and round in me head.

When I woke up I was in a cot with the bars up, in a children's ward. A cleaner mopping over the ward floor greeted me with a cheery 'Hello' and then said ' Ah, a new little one to have her tonsils out'. I became hysterical and cried until I was sick. Downstairs in the waiting room me mammy had been told they had unfortunately dropped the 'removed tooth' and I'd swallowed it!.

For the next few hours I was brought up and down to the x-ray department every half hour to make sure the swallowed tooth wasn't doing any damage, and to watch the journey it was making! Me mammy had been left sitting in the waiting room for five hours. Every so often someone would talk to her and tell her what progress was being made.

Everyone else had gone to see the film 'The Lady and the Tramp' showing on the DeLuxe Cinema in Camden Street. Me mammy promised I would be brought to see the film another time. When the crisis was over and they felt there was nothing to worry about I was allowed to go home with me mammy.

....

Chapter 29

Biting Myra!

After eventually catching up with the class we moved up to 2nd Class and me next teacher was quite a big person to me. She was called 'The nun with the press of treasures'. She was big in stature and had a red birthmark shaped like a heart upside down on her cheek. I always thought hearts stood for love, but somehow I was a little frightened of her. Her voice was as big as her stature and there was dead quiet when she was around.

She used the cane freely and everyone dreaded the Friday sums tests. Every sum that we got wrong we felt the cane across the palm of our hand. For that reason I learnt fast and by the end of the year I came 3rd in the class and was rewarded with a colouring book and pencils.

Me and Maura Smith were still treated as delicate girls by the teaching Sister and in the winter time when the open fire was lit in the classroom she used to put our little bottles of milk beside the fire to warm them. We both hated warm milk but we didn't dare say it!

There were times when I thought it would be nice to experience being hugged or even kissed but, we were a family of 'No Touching'. Even though we had to share our beds with each other, head to toe or side by side, there was an invisible line down the centre we just didn't cross, even if someone was frightened or having a bad dream.

I can't ever recall being hugged or kissed by me mammy, but I guess it is possible. I know I had a bad temper and a very short fuse. I remember having a terrible row with Myra in the bed we were sharing and I remember giving Myra a nasty bite but somehow I cannot remember what the row was about after all these years. I was unfortunately caught out: who wouldn't be? Myra's screaming could be heard all the way down Clanbrassil Street.

What I remember was my pleading, 'I'm sorry, I'm sorry' in a futile effort to try to get Myra to shut up.

Chapter 30

Gas Masks and a Mattress

One hot summer day daddy decided it was time to empty and re-pack one of the bed mattresses and we could do this in the back-yard. Out came the gas masks from their brown cardboard boxes that had been kept at the back of the wardrobe in the top shelf, everyone was standing wearing the masks making funny noises and fogging up the goggles with laughing.

The mattress was hauled down the stairs and out to the yard. Everyone stood knee-deep in mattress filling which looked like very fine black steel wool, or something similar as it was tumbled out before us. It was everywhere and the black dust billowed all around us. We had to stop every so often to de-fog our masks, have a drink and a piece of bread and then back to work loosening up the filling getting rid of the dust and putting it back in to the mattress cover. It had to be done in a day or no mattress for someone! Did everyone enjoy the messing about wearing the gas mask and the laughter? I don't know, but I did.

The wireless on the kitchen window-sill, a witness to all the happenings in the back yard, sat tuned into Radio Eireann. The wireless, our only family entertainment held everyone's attention in the evenings, especially in the winter evenings. We listened to programs such as 'The School around the Corner, Din Joe invites everyone to his ceili, with songs, dances and ballads with the Garda Ceili Band at 8pm. and Michael O'Hehir's commentary on Sport. There was a series of Detective Stories. I recall a continuous programme about Dick Turpin, who threatened the passengers in the stagecoach with a pistol in his hand shouting what sounded like "Stand on your Liver", but we were told, he actually said "Stand and Deliver" to be continued ... and 'Ghost Stories' after which no-one wanted to go to bed. There were many more late programmes into the night for big people only.

Chapter 31

Cat's Lick – Saturday Night Bath Ritual

We were kept as clean as possible with no hot water on tap. I was often enough accused in school of arriving with a face that had the markings of a cat's lick. That must have been towards the end of the week. A tide mark could be seen where the lick finished.

I wasn't too close to 'Cleanliness being next to Godliness'. Saying that, the others couldn't have been either, except those who were older of course. There was no such thing as a washing machine so all the sheets and clothes were boiled first, then hand washed and put through the wringer. There was steam coming out of the kitchen for hours.

On Saturday night there was the usual ritual of baths. The tin bath, family size, was unhooked from the back of the yard door and when everyone was young, it was placed on the kitchen table on top of a pile of newspapers to soak up the splashing, and in rotation of age we had our weekly bath. After our baths, us girls wore soft bodices under our nighties and the boys wore all-in-one combi-suits to keep them warm.

As the older ones of the family grew into young people they were looking for privacy so the bath was transferred into the scullery and big cooking pots had to be filled in the scullery with cold water, brought into the kitchen for boiling and then back to the scullery to fill the bath. Never ending journeys back and forth.

The other thing was there seemed to be a constant draught coming from under the back yard door no matter what was put against it. Our economic friendly transportable 'Alladin' paraffin oil heater was brought out to the scullery. On one occasion one of me brothers sat on it for a split second, by mistake, was left with the telltale marks on his bottom. Very painful!!

While we were having our baths, our daddy would polish all our shoes and line them up in a row in front of the range in the kitchen ready to wear. We always had clean clothes and clean shoes to wear for Mass every Sunday.

....

Chapter 32

Granny's - Mass-Misdemeanor

While young we were brought to St. Theresa's church, Donore Avenue for the Children's Mass every Sunday because our granny lived on O'Donovan's Road which was on the route to the church and we were invited to call in on our way home afterwards.

A good Catholic family was expected to bring their children to the children's Mass every week whatever the weather and we were one of those families. Between the ages of six and seven years old, boys and girls received their First Holy Communion and were expected to receive the Eucharist having fasted from midnight. If anyone was feeling faint a sip of water was the only drink that could pass their lips.

On arriving at Mass we were marched up to the front of the church to sit with the other children and we weren't allowed to talk, whisper or look around, as if we would!! The priest said the Mass in Latin of which none of us understood a word. The priest had his back to the congregation but I was sure he had eyes in the back of his head.

There was no excuse for not receiving Holy Communion or, EVERYONE would want to know why. The only bits we younger ones would have understood were the three 'Hail Mary's', the 'Hail Holy Queen' followed by 'O God our Refuge and Strength' and a prayer to 'Holy Michael Archangel' for the conversion of Russia. These prayers were said at the end of Mass as ordered by Pope Leo X111 and we all had to kneel down.

With Mass over and we were going to be good for the rest of the day (well, that was the hope). we were ready to meet our Granny, who was really the boss over all the family and everyone took advice from her, listened to whatever she had to say and we were warned not to fidget.

It had become a Sunday ritual, call to see Granny and she just might give everyone a penny. We would all traipse into the dining room and be greeted by Granny who had snow-white hair and what seemed like thousands of wrinkles on her face. Betty, Stella and Evelyn would look on as Granny inspected us to see if we were clean and that we were wearing clean knickers, "Because you never know when you might have an accident!" That was to us girls. The boy's shirt collars were also inspected. We did our mammy and daddy proud every Sunday! It was all a serious game being played out over and over again.

The reward for the visit was the gift of 1 penny each. We were not, no matter how young we were, allowed to ask for the penny and it was a sin among sins when Enda got restless, probably because she'd been kept standing too long on her bad leg or maybe she was in a brazen mood, or just being a brazen hussy, as Auntie Betty would say! anyway, she asked so everyone could go to their favourite shop and spend the 1 penny.!

There was complete silence while we listened to our granny giving a lecture about asking for money and that it was bad manners, but, she was good, she gave us the treasured penny and we left happy.

Now, the penny was worth a fortune when we only got one a week especially as we might have spent the whole week thinking about what we could buy. Ten aniseed balls or twenty sticks of liquorice, love hearts and lozenges, sherbet fizz bags, gob stoppers, lucky dips and a lot more. I could even taste them and feel me mouth water before I even got the penny. All those treasures could be bought and were sold in newspaper, shaped like a cone in that very special sweet shop.

Myra and I experienced a Sunday we would unfortunately regret. With three aunts around it was like having a grand jury and none of them were on our side.

When Myra and me were a little older and trusted to go to Mass on our own there was one Sunday when we just didn't fancy going but needed a backup story we could agree on as we knew we were expected to turn up in granny's house afterwards and there was no way we could not visit. Granny was expecting us and we always did what our granny expected!

We rehearsed the biggest lie of the year, but arrived at granny's house too early to have been anywhere near Mass. Questions, questions and more questions. Of course we tripped themselves up trying to redeem ourselves. The more we said the worst it got. We wished we hadn't got out of bed that Sunday – it was an unforgivable crime in their eyes, and was NEVER repeated.

....

Chapter 33

Our Street

Those treasured pennies earned from our granny would all be spent in May Ward's sweet shop on the corner of Clanbrissil Terrace. It was a very small, very dark mysterious place with a wooden floor and three stairs down to the counter with shelves overflowing with glass jars full of sweets. It was like finding treasure to every sweet toothed child. The choice was so vast it was mesmerizing.

Lower Clanbrassil Street was our world of shops. Geoghan's, otherwise known as 'Rocks', the grocer's shop where we could have grocery items on tick. Me mammy ran up a weekly bill where she could send one of us to ask for whatever she wanted and it was added to the bill.

It was the place where a Kennedy's Loaf of bread and a lot more besides could be bought. In a family as big as ours, the question was 'How far does a Kennedy's loaf of bread go among so many?' The slices were always counted and everyone only took what was theirs. One day mammy was clearing out the wall food press when she found 'IT'- a very hard piece of bread with a chunk of margarine on it. Someone must have been eating it when they heard a noise or something and rather than be caught with it they threw it into the back of the press and must have forgotten to go back for it. Who ever it was mustn't have counted on our mammy ever clearing out that press! The culprit (or thief - and not a good thief at that) had left a fine set of teeth marks in the margarine.

To say our mammy was cross was an understatement, because our mammy could put the fear of God into us for the least thing. So when every-one was dragged in and our teeth were measured to the teeth-marks in the bread we were prepared to die, or at least deny any knowledge of it rather than suffer the consequences! Funny that it appeared everyone's teeth marks were the same! No-one ever owned up and neither would you, if you had been there!.

I loved going into 'Rock's Shop', I was always fascinated watching Betty slice cheese. It was a real art. With great concentration she would cut a piece of greaseproof paper and place it over the cutting edge of the carving knife and proceed to cut very thin slices of cheese off a big block of Galtee cheese that had been wrapped in silver and packed in a wooden case. It was always intriguing how many slices could be got for a quarter of a pound. I could just about see over the counter where there was a meat slicer, worked by turning a handle, for perfect slices of cooked ham and corned beef, luncheon meat or hazlett.

Betty and Mrs. Rock loved a good chat with their customers. Rock's was the shop for anyone who had started smoking. Cigarettes were sold in ones if that's all the money we had in our hand, and it didn't matter what age we were. If we were sent by an adult we were served. We could even buy two ounces of broken biscuits and if our ears had been big enough we would have eavesdropped on all the secrets the adults shared.

Jacobs and Boland's fancy biscuits were all displayed in fat glass jars with silver lids and some in tins with see through glass lids. They all looked delicious and 'must have'. Everyone's favourites were Jacobs coconut creams, soft, melt in your mouth mallow in a delicate shade of pink or fluffy white on a sweet biscuit that had a secret dab of jam right in the middle underneath, and the Kimberley biscuit with its sandwich of dark brown, tasting of ginger - soft biscuits with sugary white marshmallow filling and the Mikado with it's soft biscuit underneath with pink fluffy mallow with cocoanut on top and separated down the middle with a line of jam.

Sheila, one of the big girls who lived down the lane worked in Jacobs and got a big bag of broken biscuits to take home every week. Some of us occasionally longed to be old enough to work in Jacobs. I fancied working in a sweet shop, just as I imagined every other child's wish would be if they had a sweet tooth. That was always a possibility because anyone over the age of fourteen years old who had left school could get a job in a sweet shop, a grocer shop or a factory.

....

Chapter 34

Shops And More Shops

Beyond Rocks was Larkins pub where many a child was left outside to play while their mammy and daddy were having a drink. Terry and Nuala were pals with the landlord's children as they were around the same age. And next door there was the bookies' shop Kilmartin's.

Next door to that was Luigi Pacini the Statue Maker, an Italian family who sold plaster statues and religious objects. They had a shop with a window displaying their religious statues, medals and rosary beads. Though the shop front was in Clanbrassil Street they unpacked their wooden crates of imported goods from Italy in the alley at the back of their shop, so there was straw and white dust and plenty of bits of chalk around to map out piggy beds for play. Me brother Brian and Baba Pacini were friends.

Further on was Byrne's, a small clothes shop where I would look longingly in the window, wishing and hoping that someday maybe I might be able to buy something when I got rich!.

Then there was Corcoran's the boot repairer. The Bamba bookshop owned by Seamus Fitzpatrick next door to Corcoran's sold very cheap secondhand books. There were always people coming and going for it was a great place to spend some time just reading or looking at the picture books and comics. It was always very quiet in there with people engrossed with their head in books and more books. It was like having a library close by. Finally there was Byrne's, General Draper and Wm. Walsh sold provisions.

Situated between Long Lane and Daniel Street on the left side along Lower Clanbrassil Street was a much frequented place, The Fish an Chip shop where battered fish and singles of big fat chips were sold We could watch them frying in the hot suet fat which was sold to them by the local butcher, close by, feel the heat, taste the smell that wafted around as everyone waited to be served on a cold evening. There was a happy feeling as everyone was eventually served a fresh evening meal cooked to their liking, wrapped in newspaper ready to take home.

Also to be found on that side of the street was Brerton's Grocery shop, Byrne's Dairy and Joseph Lynch's Dairy where everyone brought their own milk jug and had it filled from a big urn. Fresh cream was sold also. And then just off the Street in Harty's place was another cobbler and another Betting shop could be found in William's Place.

....

Chapter 35

Jam Jars and Lemonade Bottles

One of possibly the biggest shops named 'Somer's' was situated facing our house across the road. We never actually shopped there when we were small because the traffic was constant and dangerous. When Brian, Terry and Nuala were older they were allowed to cross the road. Mr. Somers seemed to sell everything a person could want, 1d bundle of sticks, firelighters, briquettes and turf but these items could be bought in 'O'Brien's' more or less next door to us. But we had a liking for tinned steak and kidney pies, tinned peas or beans, sliced corn beef or ham depending on what day it was.

Terry was known to collect empty jam jars and lemonade bottles and sell them to Mr. Somers who actually paid him a ha'penny for each one, only when Mr. Somer's back was turned, Terry took the jam jars and lemonade bottles back and resold them to him later in the day. Terry may have had an insight into a future career of a Salesman? He was very bold!.

Terry was our brother who joined the boy scouts and went camping with them at weekends. He worked hard to get all his badges and became the Assistant Scout Master. Ciaran later joined the 55th Scout Troop in the South Circular Road den. Towards the end of his scouting days Terry attended a few of the meetings but never in uniform. The Scout Master, Freddy Moiselle always had a good word to say about Terry.

When Terry grew out of the scouts he joined the FCA and went on maneuvers with them during holiday time and at weekends. He put long hours into spit and polishing his boots and with Brasso and cloth to shine his buttons. He took part in the Easter Parade that took the route from Griffiths Barracks down Clanbrassil Street, New Street, Patrick Street, St. Nicholas Street, past Christchurch Cathedral, down Lord Edward Street past Dublin Castle to Dame Street, following around past the Bank of Ireland on College Green, along Moreland Street into O'Connell Street to take the salute outside the GPO. Gerald and Ciaran and probably half the kids from the neighbourhood were running along-side waving and shouting just to catch his attention as the parade passed down Clanbrassil Street, but Terry was not distracted. Eyes front as though in a trance.

The money from Terry's sale and resale of jam jars and lemonade bottles went towards going to the flicks on a Saturday morning. None of us were allowed to go to the Tivoli picture house in Francis Street because it was a flee-house, so mammy said – she had her principals!

The only cinemas at that time that we and our friends were able to afford and were close enough to home was either the DeLuxe Cinema in Camden Street where there was a showing of the Film 'Here Comes Trouble' with the Extra feature being 'Pitfall' starring Dick Powell and Lizebeth Scott. Or to the 'Green' Cinema located (wait for it) at St. Stephen's Green which was featuring 'Monte Casino' with the added attraction of Abbott & Costelloe in 'Meet the Killers'. Saturday was the day when everyone would sort out their 4d and queue up for a long time before the cinema had even opened. It was no orderly queue!

....

Chapter 36

The Factory Next Door and more Shops

Next door from our house to the right, going towards Leonard's Corner, was Mulcahy's factory where they manufactured the 'Bear Brand' nylon stockings and knitwear. On special occasions or when we had a camera we would have our pictures taken standing in front of the best cars in the car park. We never played in the car park, possibly because we might have been heard, it was just too close to home.

On the far side of Mulcahy's gates at No. 98 was Mrs. O'Brien's fruit and vegetable shop, which also sold flowers and lots of other things that Mr. Somers sold over the road. On the corner of Donovan's Lane was the Bunch of Grapes pub which was a second home to many of the men, married or not married living close by. Then there was Lawler's, the clothes shop, and a little grocery shop named Fitzpatrick's that sold desiccated coconut for our school cookery lessons, otherwise known as Domestic Science!.

Going toward Leonard's Corner in the middle of the shops was the doctor's surgery up a flight of stairs in a house where our mammy would bring us if our illness was not serious enough for the hospital.

Facing these shops was Sweeney's where all the ingredients and drinks for Christmas were bought and then there were the much visited drapery shops, Staffords for nylons, blouses, skirts and cardigans and underwear, but the family could only afford nylons or socks, and because mammy knitted and could replace collars on the boys shirts with the tails of their shirts and she had friends who did some dress making for us girls, she wasn't a constant customer.

When Brian was working he would ask anyone who was willing to go for a message for him to the shops. He always paid a penny for going so they were willing goers. On one occasion he asked someone to buy him a pair of socks. They did and brought him back the right colour and the right size. Brian having a sense of humour, took the socks out of the bag, held them up in front of him, one in each hand with the heels touching and the toes going in the opposite direction and said in a very serious voice

" Sorry, but you'll have to take them back, they've given you two odd socks."

There was pandemonium because no-one liked returning anything, not even for a penny and they'd have eaten the sweets already!

Betty's for buttons and ribbons, colours, shapes, sizes, strips, cards, wool, sewing needles, threads everything you could ever want if you liked sewing!. A lot of hand sewing and darning and altering was done but not many clothes were bought. Nuala, Myra and me got to know Betty very well and she was great in helping us decide on the right hair ribbons that suited us.

Then nearer to Leonard's Corner was the Kilbride's Pawnbroker and Jeweller with the three symbolic Gold Balls hanging outside, the easily recognisable symbol anywhere in the world. The shop was painted black and every Monday a very long queue of people in need of a loan queued outside.

That was our world when we were young!

....

Chapter 37

Autumn Term

The next teaching sister to inherit the class was a softy old thing who looked rather fragile. She seemed very thin and frail looking with a lot of broken veins on her face and she wore little round glasses. She was very quietly spoken. She didn't need to raise her voice, one look and she had everyone's attention and a new term of ten weeks began.

During the Autumn Term the school closed while we celebrated Halloween. The dinner menu of the day was colcannon, specially prepared mashed potato with thrup'enny bits wrapped in greaseproof paper mixed in and this was served with boiled bacon. A very traditional Irish meal and suited to the occasion. To whoever got the money, it meant they were going to be rich (for that day anyway).

At evening tea-time there was traditional Barn Breac bread which would be covered over with a cloth while being cut just in case the knife struck the ring embedded in it, giving away it's hiding place. To whoever got the ring it meant they would get married. After tea there were games and cracking of nuts and eating of fruit and bobbing for apples in a basin of water or dangling on a string that would not stay still long enough to get even a bite out of it. We just ended up with wet faces.

The rest of the term was spent in readiness for the usual end of term tests in Maths and English and of course all thoughts were on the yearly Nativity Play and who would be picked for the leading roles? Come to that, even to be picked for the crowd scene would have been something. Nobody rushed into the class to ask me to take on the part of the Virgin Mary or even anyone else. It seemed like the usual pupils who smiled nicely and of course had ringlets in their hair, that was my reasoning, and I had neither, but I never thought the Virgin Mary would have ringlets either, but what did I know?.

As the lights went down and silence prevailed in the school hall, everyone's secret wish was to be up there on stage doing it better as they watched the Nativity story unfold year after year. It always held the same magic no matter how many time we watched it. But we loved every moment of it and applauded loud and long until our hands hurt, and we left the school hall feeling happy and secretly hoping that maybe their chance would come next time!.

Chapter 38

Christmas

As the school days rolled on to Advent which began on the 1st Sunday of December (which was ordained by the Church as the preparation time for Christmas) me mammy was busy at home getting all the ingredients for the Christmas puddings and much loved Christmas cake.

The soaking of the currents and raisins, the slicing and cubing of the sugared candied peel, the cutting of the cherries and rolling them in flour so they wouldn't sink to the bottom of the cake, the spices, the brown sugar, the flour and of course the browning and spirits: all part of Christmas as a child. The smells, the heat, everyone having a stir and making their own special wish with their eyes closed.

Then came the steaming of the puddings in their muslin cloths sitting for hours in pots of boiling water bubbling away and the window panes in the kitchen steamed up for us to draw funny faces on and a homely smell wrapped itself around us. Then followed the Christmas cake baking in the oven for hours, and us children wishing and dreaming about what we wanted for Christmas, I doubt it was what we would get but more what we wanted. We'd have written to Santy already and posted the letter up the bedroom chimney, which of course went straight to Santy as the letters were never found again by any of us.

Lastly before the school Autumn term ended prizes for best results in class tests were given out and how I did excel! It had been a long time coming.

We had two weeks off for the Christmas holidays which were not spent reading at our leisure or swaning off to do our own thing. There was the cleaning and the clearing out of every press in the house to be done, even the paintwork was washed - well 'The Devil finds work for Idle hands' so me mammy made sure there were no vacancies.

During those two weeks of icy cold and wet wintry weather the brightness shone on our faces when we were brought to see Santa Claus in McBernie's toy shop on the Quay. The shop windows held all our wishes and dreams of what we would like and we did love sitting on Santa Claus' knee and whispering what we hoped we would get.

On Christmas Eve in the afternoon all of us who had made our Holy

Communion went to confession in the Carmelite Church in Whitefrier Street. In the early evening one by one or two by two we had a bath. When we were all ready for bed we would sit in the parlour where there was a coal fire in the grate with flames licking at the chimney.

A real Christmas Tree stood in the corner to the left of the fireplace, every branch covered with very fragile silver coated, brightly coloured ornaments with lights reflecting from the Christmas Tree off the front window, giving off a festive atmosphere to the street as well as to us: it was magic. There were Christmas paper chains hanging from the ceiling and presents under the tree and there we sang carols together.

Christmas was a happy occasion. It was traditional and consistent. Christmas never changed. When all the younger ones were all finally ready we all had our tea and went to bed for what seemed the longest night of the year. Sleep did not come easy to any of us.

We stayed awake long into the night whispering, with shouts from downstairs, 'Go to sleep, Santy won't come if you are awake' but we were still hoping we might catch a glimpse of Santy through half shut eyes. We didn't. When we finally slept 'He'd' have come and gone without a sound.

Our mammy and daddy went off to midnight Mass in Whitefrier Street Church and at about 5 am Christmas morning the rest of us would wake up to our Christmas stocking at the foot of our beds. By 5.30am we were out of the house on our way to the 6am Mass at the same Church.

Christmas was the time of the year when we were dressed in new clothes and new shoes. The air was still and quiet outside, it was still dark with few people about and we could see the frost coming off our breaths as we hurried along. We were too excited and happy to feel the cold.

After breakfast everyone was allowed into the Parlour to see the rest of the presents and give each other presents we'd made or might even have bought but had kept hidden until the previous evening.

The turkey cooked through the night so everywhere in the house felt warm and there was that wonderful smell of cooking meat, roast potatoes, boiled bacon, followed by Christmas pudding and custard. Thank God for Christmas!

....

Chapter 39

His Master's Voice

Christmas was a time when we showed off our finery so off we'd go to visit our Granny. Granny's, O'Donovan Road, or Betty's and Stella's, one house, three different titles. It was really our second home.

Evelyn, Betty and Stella, me daddy's sisters lived there as well. They seemed all grown up and working by the time I became aware of them as aunties. Evelyn and Betty went to Scoil Breda and then on to The Holy Faith Convent in Clarendon Street. Stella was sent to the National School, in Weavers Square. Both Betty and Stella became turf accountants when they left school. They worked for P.J.Kilmartin around the different offices in Dublin, but their main office was in Abbey Street. Evelyn worked in the clothing Industry where she met her future husband Michael Ball.

Evelyn, Betty and Stella were the best of aunties and we had great times with them, they were always interested in everything we did. They enjoyed playing games with us and they had records and a record player. When we visited they would take out their new toy: a 'His Master's Voice' gramophone player and place it on the table so we could watch and listen but not touch.

What came out of the speaker was the most wonderful sound that filled the air in that room and could be heard all over the house until it slowed up and needed to be rewound, there were always willing hands and each of us looked longingly and pleadingly at Betty and Stella in the hope that we would be picked.

The machine was handled as though a precious jewel. The black vinyl 78s records were stored and protected in paper sleeves with just the centre label showing the name of the song and the artist's name, with a picture of a dog listening to a Gramophone. When the black vinyl record was removed from it's sleeve, it was dusted and reverently laid on the turntable. The playing needle on the end of a shining curling shaped arm was then checked to remove any fluff or dust collected and it was placed on the outer rim of the record and a pure sound arose. We never failed to be mesmerised.

We would dance around the table with Betty or Stella and Evelyn to the music of Joe Loss playing the Wedding Samba which was aunt Evelyn's favourite song, along with the voices of John Count McCormach, Mario Lanza and many, many others. Ciaran's favourite was a song called 'Little Jimmy Brown': 'O the Chapel Bells were ringing, 'twas for Little Jimmy Brown and the songs that they were singing ... Bong, Bong ...'

The gramophone was one of those wonderful inventions that brought happiness to people the world over. To us, it was pure magic!

There was a story going around some time later that the gramophone had been lent to Brian for some occasion and it was strapped to the back of his bicycle but somehow it fell off and smashed into pieces?. We can only imagine the devastation that would have caused!.

Betty had been christened Elizabeth, but the only one who called her that was our cousin Adele. Betty always corrected us when we called her Behhy. 'Its not Behhy, its Betty!' she'd say. Betty could always make us laugh by the many expressions she used to suit the situation. 'Vanity, Thy Second Name', 'You're a Brazen Hussy' or 'You're a Floosie' and of course 'Self praise is no praise'.

After the fun of listening to some music, singing and dancing on Christmas day the table was cleared for the traditional game of cards called Newmarket. Everyone in the family learnt to play cards and we learnt very quickly and, our counting of pennies improved with it.

Two packs of cards needed. Four picture cards of different suites, usually 2 Kings and 2 Queens from one deck, were placed in the middle of the table. The game was played with the second pack of cards and the dealer dealt him or herself an extra hand. No cheating was allowed: the lowest in suit (black or red, aces low) was always the lead. The spare hand to the dealer could be sold, but it appeared that Doris always had the spare hand! How? (And why?)

Money was placed on the cards in the centre, usually a penny and if you were allowed to play the matching cards you won the money on them, otherwise the amount of money on the centre cards increased for the following game. The rest of the money was the 'kitty', which went to the winner of the game.

As we each learnt to play and had reached a certain age, we were allowed to play and we became the card sharks of the future. Otherwise we just watched and kept an eye on someone's money. It was always for pennies and we always went home rich!

Christmas was also Panto time and we were taken to the Gaeity Theatre in King Street near Grafton Street once or twice over the years. We were dressed in our best clothes and we though it was great fun even if we only had seats up in the 'Gods'.

We had to lean forward and strain ourselves to see the stage with Maureen Potter and Jimmy O'Dea who complemented each in their different roles. Me memories of us singing to the words of Molly Malone, 'As she wheels her wheel Barra through streets Broad and Narra, Crying Cockles, and Mussels, Alive, Alive O'.

The Pantomimes were as much a part of Christmas as Santa was part of presents. It was great fun when like all the other kids there, we joined in the shouting 'He's behind you' and we loved it.

We all knew Maureen Potter was known to be a great person who could memorise lists of names and birthday dates and she would stand in the middle of the stage and call out the names and the rows where the birthday people were sitting and send special wishes to them, but what I know was, I never heard any of the our names being read out. But then, none of us had a Birthday in January!

....

Chapter 40

Another New Year

After the celebrations and the ringing of Christchurch Bells heralding in a brand New Year it was back to school to show off new pencil cases, pencils, rubbers, colouring pencils, pencil sharpeners, rulers, jotters and everything else we got for Christmas that we could fit into our schoolbags to show off or exchange for something different.

Another calendar year begins and the weather as cold as ever with frost and snow late January and early February. St Bridget's day, 2nd February was nearly always a day of snow and to me it seemed like the coldest time of every year: not a time to look forward to. It was also a bad time of year for Enda as she suffered from snow blindness.

The high ceiling class rooms, with enough benches to seat forty or more children and radiators which seemed to only get to 'warm' rather than 'hot' - and they were guarded with wire surrounds to protect against 'burnt fingers'.

The coal fire blazing gave little warmth because of the big windows that rattled and let in the draught. It was a time of icy cold fingers, which we tried to keep warm tucked up the sleeves of our cardigans, just like the teachers did, but they had big sleeves, we only had cardigans or jumpers. That didn't help when trying to hold a pencil. Even in the classroom everyone's breath in the air was like a fog. It was time to settle down to a new term. It was very hard to concentrate on anything when we felt so cold and there were no exceptions!

As sure as Winter is followed by Spring, the season of Christmas is followed by the celebration of Easter and again a period of preparation was required by the Church of all healthy people between the ages 21 to 60 years – we had to observe the season of Lent. Six weeks of self-sacrifice, just one full meal and two small meals every day during Lent except Sundays. Fridays were days of Abstinence from meat.

Before Lent begins there is a party of pancakes, with the smell of freshly squeezed lemons, the sprinkling of sugar and a lot of tossing pancakes in the air for the celebration of Shrove Tuesday: the feast before the famine. The smoking of a well-used frying pan filling the air added to the atmosphere.

Six weeks giving up sweets (but often just hoarding them instead.) Just because we all promised to give up *eating* sweets, didn't mean we didn't buy them. We saved them for St. Patricks Day, which was a Holyday of Obligation, a Bank Holiday and a Day of Celebration, when a parade of mobile floats advertising every organization and every shop in the form of grandiose displays, wheeled past with people waving flags or throwing sweets. It was always a great day to be off school.

Our real Penance for Lent was that it was going to be the season of 'Bulls Eyes' again! Those black and white striped boiled sweets that stuck together in a paper bag when kept too long lying in a warm pocket. 'Oh No, Not the Bulls Eyes Sweets, 40 Days Bull's Eyes Diet for Daddy!!

Every year we secretly hoped. 'No, not this year, but yes, suck, without fail, suck, for as long as we could remember, unfortunately, suck, hard work ahead, suck, suck. It was going to be another dry and Smoke-Free Lent for daddy and a busy, 'Don't Say A Word' quiet one for everyone else.

Out came the dungarees, the paint and brushes, the smell of turpentine, rags, jam jars, wallpaper and paste and the sharing of basins of water to wash the woodwork AGAIN!!

The wallpaper on the walls already was not removed but another heavy duty embossed layer was put on top to reinforce the wall underneath the many covers of wallpaper and linoleum to keep the damp out. On the ceiling were a few coatings of wallpaper also just to keep the heat in or possibly to keep the ceiling from falling down. It was all very hardwearing for the wear and tear of a large family. It was just the kitchen that was wallpapered every year and we all secretly thanked God!.

The sitting room cum parlour was used only on special occasions so didn't need decorating every year as that was where we had our meals when the kitchen was being decorated. Otherwise we would have needed an extended Lent and no-one would have wanted that!.

School closed for Easter holidays the Friday before Holy Week. On Maundy Thursday every Catholic Family keeps up the tradition to visit seven churches, so off we'd go to the parish churches of St. Teresa's, Donore Ave, St. Kevin's, Harrington Street, St Nicholas of Myra, Francis Street, St Catherine's, Meath Street, The Carmelite Church in Whitefrier's St., St Augustin's, Thomas Street and Adam and Eve's on the quays, and then made the round of the Stations of the Cross.

Everyone was also asked to keep the silence on Good Friday between 12 noon and 3pm, so it was a very quiet day in the Lane, as we sat or held up someone's window sill in the sun and read a book instead. The day always seemed to be warm and sunny but a discreet eye was kept on the sky during those silence hours, to see if it would become dark!.

As children we wouldn't have gone to the Easter Saturday night services but there was the family tradition of the older artistic brothers and sister boiling an egg for each of us, wait for them to cool, paint funny faces on them, giving them a name for each of us younger brothers and sisters.

Not everyone was pleased with the outcome when the eggs had names like, Cry Baby 1 or Cry Baby 2 ... We had to eat the boiled egg before we could eat our Easter egg.

••

Chapter 41

Processions

A big part of life in Dublin were the May Processions to our Lady. For four Sundays in every year Nuala brought me and Myra with her from the time we could walk to school, to Mount Argus Church near Harold's Cross to take part in the processions on Sunday afternoons. These outings are not remembered with fondness or enjoyment but we weren't given a choice. Once we made our First Holy Communion we were the proud owners of white dresses and veils so we could truly take part. Enda wasn't brought because she couldn't walk that far.

I especially dreaded being stuck in the church for all those hours. We would arrive shortly after dinner, hours before it was due to start or so it felt. We would sit, sit and sit while nothing was happening, all we could do was swing our legs, fiddle with our veils or dresses or spend the time fidgeting as we were only allowed to read prayer books in church and well they weren't very interesting.

Mount Argus was a very big church with lots of grounds to walk around. The Church was split, with two rows down the centre aisle and then one row all the way down left and right at the sides. I think we were put in the same place every time on the right side near the confessional boxes where nothing was going on that we could see. We never made it to the centre seats or we might have seen something that might have made it more exciting or more interesting for us.

All the brightly coloured banners identifying the church's fraternities were on display, surrounded by brass rings to keep them up standing to attention at the edge of the centre aisle seats. I began to think that maybe our dresses were not 'Persil White'® enough for the centre benches???

The whole event seemed to take hours to organise and all we heard from behind were the people shushing us up when we talked too loud or giggled. I just wanted to be out in the sunshine playing.

Eventually we were led from our pew and told to follow the long straggling line of people going outdoors. We dragged our feet in a slow walk and sang in our loudest voices and rattled off the 'Our Father's, Hail Mary's and Glory B's, which could only have sounded painful, but God gave us those voices!.

We sang hymns to Our Lady, 'O Mary we crown Thee with blossoms today, Queen of the Angels and Queen of the May'; I'll Sing a hymn to Mary, the Mother of my God; Ave, Ave, Ave Maria , Ave, Ave, Ave Maria; Purest of Creatures, Sweet Mother. Sweet Maid; Hail Queen of Heaven, the Ocean star! Guide of the wanderer here below.

Babies crying, toddlers dragging behind and some of them being carried by the student, would be priests in their long black robes, rattling rosary beads and white soutans. They also kept an eye on everyone to make sure we didn't go missing along the way.

When we finally made it out into the sunshine the procession came down the church steps, past the grotto of Our Lady, then went through the church grounds across the little bridge, around the back and finally back to church. The procession was followed by Benediction back in the church.

The sun seemed to always shine so there was no excuse for not being there. I was so glad when the afternoons came to an end and we could go to Harold's Cross Park and have a few minutes on the swings and look for frogs in the pond. There was still a long walk after that to get home.

The Corpus Christi and Christ the King processions were much more fun and enjoyable. These were like walks of celebration. Everyone who could walk took part and walked the streets carrying their church banners. The Children of Mary walked proudly wearing their blue Mantles and all sang to their hearts content. Along the way up Nicholas Street, along High Street down Cornmarket meeting up with Francis Street and back to the church.

There were shrines in people's windows and on outside window sills everyone prayed or sang with us as we walked along. There were banners and buntings all across the roads and everyone was happy. Those who weren't taking part would bring out their chairs, sit and watch and pray, their rosary beads never far away.

Not to be outdone even the school had processions around the convent grounds. It was always considered essential for growing children to take part in the school procession. It was also the only time we were allowed into the convent grounds. The children of Mary, who were all in the Secondary Classes got another chance to wear their blue cloaks, white veils and display their medal of Our Lady on a blue ribbon around their necks over their cloaks.

Each class sister kept close to her girls to see there was no giggling or talking, but there was always the usual pulling hair and undoing of ribbons and sniffing and coughing and of course someone being pulled out of line for some fault or other and she would have to walk with sister, that was punishment enough! The reward for the afternoon was usually to be let off early or no homework!

I went on two pilgrimages with the school that left lasting impressions. We went on a train to Knock, the carriages were full and decades of the rosary was recited over and over, it was relayed over the loudspeaker in each carriage and we also sang hymns to Our Lady. When the Sister who was in charge wasn't in the carriage the singing and praying was done between mouthfuls of bread or biscuits and a lot of laughing, talking and messing around was going on. We, the girls, didn't behave angelically and we didn't pretend to be saints.

Claremorris Station was the terminus so everyone had to walk the rest of the way to the Grotto. We were lucky, it was all outdoors and it was a nice day, where we recited more prayers and sang more hymns before Benediction and on the journey back.

The other Pilgrimage was to Drogheda to see the head of Blessed Oliver Plunkett, that was a journey by train also and that was a lovely day as well except I was sure I would have bad dreams after seeing the skull of Blessed Oliver Plunket being displayed in the plastic container outside in the church grounds.

....

Chapter 42

Myra and Enda

Myra, two yours younger than me, was catching up fast. She had a big smile and was a very vibrant person. She took up violin lessons with Mrs. Geraghy on Saturday mornings. Her practicing at home was not appreciated by any of us, but practice she did. She stayed with it and played at the concerts in Warrenmount school hall with her fellow players.

One year me mammy decided to enter Myra and me for the Irish speaking test for a place in the Gaelteacht Summer School in Connemara as we'd never been and me daddy couldn't afford to send us. Myra was very good but I was so nervous I became tongue-tied. We received a Missal each as a prize as we hadn't qualified for a place.

Enda, four years younger had a great spirit despite her having had polio and enduring so many operations and being in Clontarf hospital during the summer months when the rest of us were off school. I was only brought to visit her once and there she was sitting up in bed on a veranda in the sun, all smiles.

When Enda was discharged from hospital she was back at school with us in the playground, skipping and running around taking part in all the playground games. Many a broken caliper followed. Polio did not stop her doing anything she wanted. In fact people used to admire her get up and go attitude.

....

Chapter 43

Would Be Stars – Nightmares

During our school years in Warrenmount we had elocution classes with Miss Carroll once or twice a week. Our aunties Betty and Stella used to comment on our Clanbrassil Street accent all the time that even I was becoming paranoid about it. We also attended 'The Marie Kenny School of Elocution' which was held in a basement room in Harcourt Street.

Marie lived down the Lane with her sister Pauline, her brother Tim and her mammy. Her mammy was great at dressmaking. Marie had very good diction, she used to say 'Yee' instead of 'You' and to our friends' mammies and our mammy's ears, Marie sounded posh, so most of the kids in the lane attended her classes as well. There was a good attendance at Marie's club. There was some rivalry when we weren't given the parts we liked and we would get upset and not want to go.

When we weren't happy the way things were going we would sulk a little and lose enthusiasm, but we were open to being bribed with promises of cherished parts that were made for us in the current play or a place at the front of the stage for our dancing.

We took our time in deciding to make our point. But true to her word, we got parts in the play and were dressed in the hand-made costumes made by the wonderful Mrs. Kenny.

Elocution wise our Dublin accents didn't seem to improve outside the club but we got the chance to be on stage and we felt like we were stars in our own rights. It didn't matter that we didn't gain any recognition from anyone, it was all great fun and worth all the rehearsals. I was given the part of 'Sneezy' in Snow White and the Seven Dwarfs show which was held in the Father Matthew Hall, there was a great audience. We also performed in shows singing and dancing in Gardiner Street Hall. Brian was often called to play a piece of music on his violin at very short notice, sometimes he would be asked to present a cheque to a charity. There was many a night when not enough money was collected to even cover any costs but a cheque would be presented never the less.

It was the night after the last performance concert I woke up in a sweat. I had a terrible nightmare. There was the devil trying to drag me off the stage, and he just wouldn't go away and I was afraid and cried and cried.

Me mammy and daddy took me in to their bed and me daddy told me to say the Hail Mary any time I saw the Devil and the Devil would go away because the Devil didn't like people saying prayers! The Devil certainly took a lot of persuading because every time I closed me eyes he was still there. I prayed like I never prayed before: it was like the worst night of me life, I was really frightened.

Covered in spots the following morning told the story, I had caught chicken pox. When I was better and the spots were gone me mammy and daddy tried to dissuade me from going on the stage again because there might be something in the dream, but not me, I just loved the atmosphere, the make-up, the rehearsals, the singing and dancing. I did enjoy belonging to the Marie Kenny School for Elocution. I learnt later it was officially called The St. Francis Dramatic and Variety Group.

At various times during each year Marie Kenny used to hold Speaking and Poetry Competitions for Prizes, which the parents attended to see how well everyone was getting on and they were probably the only times in the whole year everyone spoke in their 'Elocution' voices. Even on those occasions I couldn't win a prize. Our cousins from Synge Street used to attend as well but for some reason I didn't know them very well.

Enda was put in the back row to hide her caliper but Myra was jealous because she thought that meant Enda was taller than her as it was usually only the tall people who were put at the back and Myra wanted to be at the back.

Before the St. Francis Dramatic and Variety Group closed for the summer Marie and her mammy would take everybody on the train for a day at the seaside as a special treat. It was usually to Seapoint. It was always a great day but we always managed to get sunburnt and then we would spend the next 'Don't touch my sunburn' in agony days. No one got any sleep we were so hot and the thoughts of someone putting calamine lotion on, brought great cries from us. All because when we went swimming we ran around without drying ourselves afterwards so got burnt but by the time holidays and seaside outings time came around again the sun-burnt affair would be forgotten.

....

Chapter 44

Summer Term – Drill Displays

No school year would have been complete without some kind of competition or fun events. The highlight of school days in Warrenmount was the three day event of their legendary drill and dancing displays.

Every class had PE twice a week all year round in preparation for this momentous event and special trainee teachers were brought in from Lyng College in Mount Street to instruct and give demonstrations of what was expected of the pupils. I enjoyed these classes most of all.

Doing exercises, playing with hoops and beanbags and running races in the hall were all in the scheme of things. In secondary there were a few ardent admirers of those young trainee teachers with their very short green PE skirts and lemon tops and everyone just knew they kept their hanky in their knickers. Who ever heard of people with pockets in their knickers? Well they must have had. Everyone could see their green knickers as the girls were performing their exercises on the floor and the teachers were directing the exercises from the stage in the school hall.

Many is the time during the summer evenings when some girls would walk up and down Mount Street hoping to catch a glimpse of their favourite PE teachers at their college as they sat with their windows open chatting to each other.

The drill displays showed the final results of a whole year's preparation. The display was coordinated by Mrs. Keaveney and Miss Walker was in charge of the Irish dancing. This grandiose display was held outdoors, nearly always in the school playground. Hours were spent by willing hands (and some not so willing hands, setting up school desks and wooden benches on three sides of the playground for the adoring parents and friends, and, many fans of certain secondary school pupils. The age range of the children was three to leaving years in secondary.

There was always an air of excitement among the girls as they practiced their dances and flag and hoop movements. They loved to twirl about in their full or dirndl skirts to see how many of their underskirts (made of stiff white mesh curtain material) would show.

The event would begin with a parade of the complete school in order of sizes and classes with the babies aged three and upwards, dressed in navy gymslips, white blouses, and many a white ribbon on shiny hair waving in the air as they walked with arms swinging. The audience could be heard making sounds of 'Aah' and possibly a tear in their eye as they clapped loud and long. The boys looked very smart in their navy shorts, white shirts, school tie and white runners. There never were such innocent looking children as seen on those occasions.

After the walk on of the whole school, a dance display and drill routines using flags, ribbons, hoola hoops and beanbags followed and each class excelled each other in excellence and expertise as they entertained their proud parents and visitors who applauded and wolf-whistled to show their appreciation.

The Finale was a scene from an Irish Legend Story led by the secondary girls looking all grown up. Every year seemed to be hot, bright and sunny. We guessed it was all due to the praying each class did every day.

One of Warrenmount School rules was, young ladies, (which must have meant us) were not allowed to wear their hair in a ponytail. 'Only Ponies have Pony-tails', was the constant reminder to all. But once or twice at home 'someone' would suggest me hair would look better in a ponytail.. The 'someone' just fancied doing a little hairdressing during their lunch-hour! I would be near to crying as me hair was being yanked back from me face and forced into an elastic band. I knew and everyone else knew the consequences! So the pony-tail didn't remain in for long, it didn't survive even as far as the school gate! I was too afraid to challenge the sister in charge or be challenged by her.

....

Chapter 45

The Many Talented

Fadle Alley was a plot of wasteland off Clanbrassil Terrace, but was turned into a place of excitement as the kids from the Lane and us put a 'Concert' together every year during the never-ending glorious hot summer holidays. Everyone spent many happy hours down The Lane, which was a haven of freedom for all.

We practiced like mad all the dances we knew and made up short plays. We set about making costumes and borrowing blankets and sheets for the stage curtains and dressing spaces. Absolutely no one was allowed a preview or a peek and everyone had to pay to watch even if they did lend their chairs to sit on to make this possible. Nothing was too much trouble. Anyone who wasn't taking part was charged one penny and the children a ha'penny.

The girls excelled in dances like 'She wore red feathers'and a Hoola, Hoola Skirt' and I'm a Little Dutch Girl/Boy, Tulips from Amsterdam. We were very inventive, open to advice and listening to others for tips. A lot of this inspiration was drawn from what we were doing at school and acts we had performed from when we attended Marie Kenny's Club

Everything that was needed to advertise this event was handmade and the local shops did good business in crepe paper, pompoms, ribbons and bits and pieces. Everyone had a hand in making and put up buntings to let everyone know it was happening. It was always a great success and we surprised everyone with our expertise and management of the Annual Summer show.

The money collected went towards a party of lemonade, and lots of cakes made by me mammy. Everyone loved her cakes: butterfly cakes were her specialty. The party was usually at our house because we had a big kitchen. There was a great atmosphere and excitement among us during this time and we thrived on new ideas with enthusiasm.

When we weren't practicing for anything in particular we played games such as Doctors and Nurses, Teacher and Pupils, Fathers and Mothers, Cops and Robbers, Cowboys and Indians and we would be seen with old sweeping brushes borrowed from someone's home sweeping our get-a-way routes or marking out our territory that was part of our make belief house.

When the kids from Malpas Place and New Street came hanging around the stone throwing would start. When I was hit on me little finger by a stone I went running off crying.

Skipping was a great game so at the corner of the alley we'd start a line for skipping with one rope and then two and do all the fancy bits. We thought we were great. We played piggy beds. Our 'beds' were drawn with a piece of chalk from one of Mr. Pacini's left over statue chalk and with the throw of 'the piggy', a shoe polish tin full of sand we'd hop on one foot from one numbered space to another picking up the 'piggy' on the way without falling or stepping on the lines. Everyone took turns.

We bought and swapped all kinds of marbles and rolled them down the gully and against the walls. When we had money we bought and swapped picture scraps and stuck them into jotters and scrapbooks. When Maura Smith and me got bored we would stand at the top of the Lane taking down the licence numbers of the cars that went up or down. (What a useful exercise!) Can there have been that many cars?.

We learnt all the rhymes off by heart, One little, two little, three little Indians ... ten little Indian boys/girls. One a penny, two a penny hot cross buns ... We played with two balls against the wall and moved on to play with three balls ... singing '1, 2, 3, O'Leary, 4, 5, 6, O'Leary 7 O'Leary, catch the ball.' Then we practiced juggling with four balls: that was more difficult.

When the evenings seemed endless we would stay out a little longer and play statues and O'Grady Said, do this, O'Grady said do that. If they said 'Do This', 'Do That', and someone moved, that was the end of the game for them.

Practicing twirling, going round and round to see who could go on the longest without getting dizzy was dangerous even though we were warned and I went smash into the corner of Mulcahy's wall and split me head open. The blood flowed and everyone around paniced. I was rushed home with everyone trailing behind and me daddy suggested someone should take me to the hospital.

But, AS IT HAPPENED, there was a 'Football Commentary ' on the radio and everyone was listening and no one wanted to miss the football, so no one brought me. I didn't mind not going. The bleeding did stop eventually, the cut did heal and I was none the worse for the accident.

Also sharing 'our' Alley were the men who played toss ha'penny. None of us took any notice of them - they were just there. But when there was a lot of money on the ground one of the boys from the Lane would run to a public telephone and ring the Gardai. When the Gardai arrived the men just scattered and the boy would run and collect the money and spend it when the men were gone. On occasions some of the men would stop and pick up a baby and pretend he was 'daddy'. None of our daddies were ever part of those gambling sessions, as we would have recognised them.

The Alley also had its own personal flasher who worked on the building site when they were building the extension to Mulcahy's Nylon Stocking Factory. The flasher paid one penny to anyone who would stroke 'IT'. All the children were sworn not to tell anyone and we never did. The kids went off happily to spend their penny.

∙∙∙

Chapter 46

Sisters, Sisters…Swimming in Sandymount

There was great rivalry between Enda, Myra and me as we were close in age and nearly the same height. A friend of our mammy was a dressmaker so we got to wear the same dresses in the same colour material but with trimmings in different places. I was not impressed because I was the oldest. I think me mammy liked people to think we were triplets!.

Enda and Myra caught up with me very quickly and Enda was tall for her age and someone told her that if she hadn't had polio she would have been the tallest! We spent a lot of time together whether indoors or outdoors which wasn't always such a good idea because we were all completely different in character.

I was given the new clothes, dresses or skirts when me mammy had money to buy them, or was given them or had them made, because I was careful, well I wasn't doing anything, was I?

The dresses especially were then passed to Myra and if there was still wear in them and they fitted Enda she got them. Enda was very hard on clothes because the many buckles on her caliper used to get caught in her skirts and dresses and tear them when she was skipping or jumping which she loved to do.

There were days during the long summer holidays when me mammy would decide to bring us to Sandymount Beach which was supposed to be our favourite place within walking distance, for a day out, if anyone would consider a walk there and back, within walking distance of our home?!

The three youngest rode in the pram and the older ones would be hanging on to the pram walking along side or running ahead. On more than one occasion the trip didn't take place because Brian managed to break his arm! When we went the route taken was along the canal. God knows how long it took to walk it. We got our training walking to and from Scoil Bride.

It would have been a natural sight to see a pram loaded with bread and jam sandwiches, bottles of drinks, kids, towels and swimsuits, out walking. Me brothers dressed in brown corduroy shorts to their knees and open necked shirts, me and me sisters in cotton dresses. When we finally arrived the chances of catching sight of the sea was rare. The sea seemed to be always at low tide so there was little chance of drowning but it didn't stop the fun feeling of arriving.

The day would be spent playing in the sand, running about or just enjoying the freedom. It was a wonderful beach and appeared to stretch on forever. I really enjoyed those carefree days when everyone seemed happy. I would walk what seemed like miles along that sand.

Me mammy's complaint was I was never within hearing distance when it was time to go home. Someone had the job of running after me and screaming their head's off for me to come back.

With the tide always appearing to be a mile or so out there was also little chance of anyone ever getting a chance to swim but, mammy would pack the swimming things and towels. The one time she decided not to bother packing any swim things the tide was only halfway out, so we all went for a paddle splashing in the shallow waves, which led to everyone jumping in it and getting wet up to our necks. The older ones walked the long miles home in damp clothes, which eventually dried on them, salt and all.

....

Chapter 47

Learning to swim with Daddy.

Our daddy was a great believer that all of us children should be able to swim so he took the lead in trying to teach each of us in turn how to swim.

One of our daddy's favourite haunts was Bray and he loved swimming so he would lead any one of us who was trusting enough, into the sea by the hand and walk with us until the water was up to our waist. he would then put one hand under our chin so we wouldn't swallow any seawater and with his other hand supporting our chest, he'd say 'I've got you, kick your legs, swim', but just after a few minutes he would take his hands away and we would sink, swallow seawater and feel sick. Disgusting!

After a few tries but with little trust in our daddy's technique, we went off and succeeded for ourselves. Some unfortunately never learnt to swim. It hadn't been a good experience!

We were very lucky to have a choice of two swimming baths, one in Tara Street and the other named Iveagh Trust Public Baths on Bride Road. Both were on the South side of Dublin and just about everyone went swimming there. Most times those of us who could or thought we could swim went to Iveagh Baths.

It seemed like hundreds of children would be pushing and shoving for a half hour swimming session. The noise was deafening. The queues seemed miles long but everyone persevered and loved the jumping and splashing. There wasn't much room for swimming, there were so many children using the pool at the same time. There was the constant blowing of whistles, life-guards waving their arms, pointing their fingers with hardly anyone taking any notice. Everyone went home dragging dripping wet towels behind them.

The Beano in Bull Alley Street was a short walk on the way home from Iveagh Baths. It was a type of club for the poor people of Dublin. It was a place we were forbidden to go to but we went ONCE! We were given cocoa and a current bun and we were allowed to join in the games and make a few 'crafty' things. I didn't like the cocoa and I was afraid someone would recognise us and go and tell our daddy so we didn't go again. We were not allowed to think we were poor!

The Baeno closed in 1962.

Chapter 48

The RDS Ballsbridge,

Daddy's yearly treat to us was a day at the horse show in the RDS Ballsbridge, Dublin 4. We'd set off early with a packed lunch and drinks for this great day. Arrive just as the queues were beginning to form and there was always a reduced rate for families or possibly me daddy actually knew someone who worked there!

Working in the hotel business he seemed to know a lot of people and now and again got seats for shows. The weather was nearly always guaranteed to be fine as it was during the summer holiday time so we were dressed in our best clothes with our faces shining and we were part of the very grand people who turned up in their best hats.

When we finally got through the front doors and were shown into the exhibition hall all we could see were hundreds of numbered stands that we would walk around, picking up as many leaflets as was possible. It was like a competition to see which one of us could collect the most. Any free giveaways there were, we got and sometimes we even found some food-stands with nice people giving out free samples. The adults on the stands seemed to be very nice to children even though they knew they weren't going to get any business from them.

At about one o'clock we would have our picnic lunch sitting on the grass outside the tent where the posh people were having their lunch and sometimes daddy would buy us some sponge cake. We were near enough to hear the brass band playing and I wistfully hoped some day I would sit in the tent. I just loved the sound of the brass band and I always felt happy there.

On one occasion Terry got lost but wasn't missed until over the loudspeaker an announcement was made. 'A little boy named Terence Mc Sweeney has been found, can the parents of this child come and collect him from the office on the first floor please?'

It was only then we looked around and Terry was not in sight, but a 'found' Terence McSweeney?. Daddy made his way to the office and there was Terry smiling. People used to call him Terence McSweeney so he thought it was his name.

In the afternoon we were brought out to where the show jumping was taking place and our daddy would miraculously produce tickets for the Final Show Jumping round for the Aga Khan Cup. One year they were even for seats! We all clapped as hard as everyone else when hearing, 'Another clear round, no faults'. After the show jumping we were taken back to the stables to see the winning horses and their rosettes.

On some evenings at home we would hear music and lots of laughing and singing when daddy had a night off and he invited his and mammy's friends and some relations to our home. Our daddy would play his violin, beginning with his signature tune 'I'll Take you home again Kathleen' on his violin, and then he would sing, but we weren't allowed to stay up.

The McNamara's were always invited, and lots of other friends that we tried to guess the names of. They always proved to be great parties and without fail we would hear Mr. McNamara tuning up for his rendering of ' Me name is McNamara, I'm the leader of the band ... Arrah you're only joking, ar rah go on you're pulling me leg, ar ... rah go on you're only joking, ar rah go on go on go on, you're pulling me leg!' Arthur Hall from Harold's Cross and John & Peggy Fitzpatrick were there also.

The front door and all the windows were all opened on the warm summer nights so there was no sleep even if sleep was needed, and all the neighbours could hear, including us upstairs who were supposed to be sleeping. We would eventually drift off.

....

Chapter 49

Myra's Red Ribbon

Our summer days were not always happy days. Nuala as big sister always seemed to have a lot of responsibility for all who were younger than her. Nuala was the one who took Myra and me to museums and galleries to get us away from the Lane and the house.

On one such day mammy gave her the money for the bus as we were going into town. Off the three of us went holding hands, Nuala, always in the middle holding on to us. Whenever we went we would get the bus there and during the day would spend the return bus-fare and walk home.

On one of those trips we were walking home along College Green on a lovely day outside the Bank of Ireland when out of nowhere came a screaming woman straight at us and made a grab for Myra's red ribbon. The woman was like a wailing banshee shouting and screaming, 'Give me that red ribbon, I want that red ribbon, its mine, it's mine' and she went on and on trying to get it but Nuala was keeping her at arms length by stepping backwards from her. Myra and me stood there frightened, clinging and crying, with Nuala trying to protect us.

People came from everywhere to help and moved between the woman and us, someone suggested Nuala put the red ribbon in her pocket and just keep walking and some of the people walked with us up Dame Street reassuring us that it was OK, not to look back, just keep going and that the woman was gone. I wanted to look back but I was afraid. I wanted to tell everyone everything that happened on that terrible day but I couldn't and Myra and Nuala couldn't because we shouldn't have spent the bus fare on sweets and we would have been safe on a bus!. I didn't know about Myra and Nuala but I had nightmares night after night and I was afraid to close me eyes as that angry woman's face seemed to just stare at me.

....

Chapter 50

Here is the News

1) This is the year when The flying of the Tricolour Flag was banned on the occasion of the unveiling in Co Antrim of a 15 foot Limestone Cross that had been erected in memory of Roddy McCorley, a young leader who was hanged on the Bridge of Toombe for being involved in the 1798 Rising.

2) Good trading in the Cattle Market with 8cwt. bullocks selling at £44 each, but at the same time a Public Health Order was considering the unhealthy effect of Street Cattle Fairs on the public highway. 'They' said, Cattle Fairs were becoming a dangerous health hazard because animal filth was being carried into shops, restaurants and houses causing food contamination. Twenty suspect cases of TB were reported under the Bovine, Tuberculous Order and six cattle had been slaughtered. It was time to abolish the primitive custom and develop a National Health consciousness through Health Education.

3) On the 19 October Pauline Ashmore aged 6 months was snatched in Camden Street and on December 20, Patrick Berrigan, a nine month old baby was snatched from his pram outside a shop at 5.15pm. On information received the Gardai's search took them to Belfast to the house of Mr. & Mrs. Geehan where Partick was found but also a little girl Elizabeth Brown who had been snatched as a baby but was then aged 4 years. There was no news on Pauline Ashmore.

4) A piece of Good News for the workers of Summerhill Engineering Co. Ltd: the new 1955 Bond Minicar is being assembled and completed at the Dublin Car Works.

5) In November of that year there was The Inauguration of a Dublin Fairyland in the City Market of Georges Street to the fanfare of trumpets – 12,000 lights came on.

6) The news from the Vatican in Rome on 3 December was that the

Holy Father Pope Pius XI (aged 78) was gravely ill after a heart attack but the news on December 4th was that He was greatly improved.

Chapter 51

Bad News on the Weather Front

High winds and gale gusts brought on the worst flooding in Ireland since 1880. It was indeed a bad year. Roads were blocked. Homes had to be evacuated due to driving rain, blinding snow and wind gusts of up to 65 miles an hour completely upsetting telegraph and electrical communications and causing wholesale flooding. The railway bridge spanning the Tolka and East Wall Road collapsed, cutting off communication between Dublin and Belfast.

The Tolka river overflowed at Botanic Avenue and poured along the avenue to Drumcondra. The worst of the flooding was around Fairview which looked like a lake. People and their possessions had to be evacuated from many parts of Dublin from Finglas, Ballyfermot, Chapelelizard and other areas where they were taken to safety and higher grounds by small boats as the water continued to rise. The rain continued in to December but it didn't affect the Dublin Cattle Market. There was a market for everything that was offered even if the numbers were down from the previous week.

Some frivolous pieces/advertisements in the papers that year –

1) 1,689 Film Stars (9 out of 10) use Lux Toilet Soap – 'You too can be Lovelier' says Susan Hayward, the 20th Century Fox, Star of the film : The Snows of Kilimanjaro.

2) 'A Tale of 2 Silhouettes' by Cassidys – Describing their Winter Coats. A wing away velvet with trim and a Cassidy creation of woolen cloth, Donegal Tweed.

3) There was the Annual Sale of Work being held in the Mansion House in Aid of The Oblate Fathers Missionary Fund.
And Finally -
4. 'Nothing in this Whole Wide World equals the Contentment that follows a wonderful meal of Donnellys skinless sausages at only 2/- for 12!

This advertisement was seen in every newspaper on sale and there was a

Lit Neon Sign on a building high up on the wall facing O'Connell Street with 'Don' tossing a Sausage to 'Nelly', back and forth, 24 hours a day.

I was not amused. The sad thing about that was 'The Donnelly Sausage Manufacturers weren't related to the Donnelly's at 100 Lower Clanbrassil Street, but when kids were being spiteful they would shout after us – 'Donnelly Sausages'!

....…...

Chapter 52

A Wedding – A Sister - A Present From Santa to Gerald

Auntie Evelyn married Michael Ball. It was a splendid affair and they were very much in love. Only adults were invited. Aileen was the youngest family guest there with Granny, Betty, Stella, Pearse and his wife Doris, Mrs. Woodford, our Daddy and Mammy, unbeknownst to some of us was the fact that me mammy was also pregnant. I wondered if Evelyn had, had her favourite music 'The Wedding Samba' by Joe Loss played at her reception, but didn't ask?.

Wedding photo 1954
L-R back row :Doris, Pearse, Evelyn and Michael, Auntie Betty, Leo (Daddy) and Aileen (Big Sister)
L-R front row: Rachel(Mammy), Frances (Granny), Mrs Woodford and Auntie Stella

Later that year when I was eleven years old, was an arrival I remembered. Rachel: another sister to the family! Why were we all surprised? Because Gerald was nearly five years old and the rest of us had been born within a year or two years of each other and we thought our mammy was too old!

On the night in question, all us young ones were woken in the early hours of a cold December night and brought down to the kitchen where the fire in the grate was still burning and it was lovely and warm where we sat with Nuala, Terry, Brian, possibly Aileen?. Gerald was already asleep.

All was quiet as everyone was lulled by the sound of the voice of someone telling a story and the warmth of the bread and sweetened milk drink. Out of the night's quietness we heard a baby cry, and the grins appeared on our faces as we looked at each other and we were immediately wide awake, except Gerald, who slept on. The mystery unfolded, the lovely Rachel had made a safe arrival, bringing the total number of us Donnellys to ten! Four boys and six girls. Lucky for me mammy, the mid-wife, Nurse Davidson only lived across the road at number 25. Nurse Davidson would have been the first person to see every new baby's face that she'd delivered on Clanbrassil Street and around the area. She had been a frequent visitor to all the families around, carrying her little black bag. I could never understand why it always seemed to be at night when she decided to deliver these babies. Now the Donnelly family could pride themselves on being the largest family in the street, I doubt if that was any consolation to me mammy. Nuala had to take the following day off school when she should have been taking a cooking exam, Nuala worried about how her partner would manage without her. No one else had an excuse to have the day off.

It was a very exciting time: a new little sister after two brothers and everyone was that little bit older to enjoy this new arrival.

A well known story that was repeated over the years was: The morning after Rachel arrived she was introduced to Gerald. Because she had been born on 19 December 1954, so close to Christmas, Gerald was told that Rachel was an early Christmas present from Santa Clause. He didn't think that was very funny but looked very sad and confused until he saw everyone was laughing and telling him they were only joking. Nuala in all but name became the mammy to our new baby sister and nursed our mammy until our mammy was ready to take over again. Nuala was the eldest girl in the family living at home but she still had to go to school. A lot of responsibility was passed on to Nuala.

I'm not sure if Rachel ever slept in the family pram that had stood under the windowsill in the kitchen all the years that the babies had been born or whether she had been issued with a more up to date model!. The family pram which had been occupied for many a year had a big deep body, black in colour with a gold design on the sides, a black hood and wheels. It was big enough to fit more than one little one, and if anyone was going anywhere we were never given the chance to go out alone: there was the usual cry from me mammy as soon as we attempted to go out to play 'Take the baby with you, and don't leave the baby on it's own!!'

On one occasion I didn't want to take the baby out, (sorry baby, to whichever baby it was) I wanted to go out on me own. The Lord said, 'Thou shalt honour thy mother and do what you're told' Well, I didn't want to. I wasn't given a choice so, I banged the pram against the walls in temper on the way out along the hall but before I had a chance to open the front door me mammy gave me a wet hand smack across me bottom. Me mammy had been doing the washing!.

It was quite normal to have to mind two or three younger brothers or sisters, but there was one boy in the lane who took delight in taking one of them back to me mammy saying he found him/her on their own, down the lane, so one of us would be in trouble with me mammy when she wouldn't believe us that we didn't leave them on their own! We would end up fighting with the kid. We didn't like him at all.

••

Chapter 53

Gerald's First Day at School –
Ciaran and Fireworks.

As Rachel made her debut into the family Gerald was starting in the Lower Babies class in Warrenmount. Leaving home was not a good day for him. He cried in the playground and didn't want to stay, possibly because he had been mothered by everyone, him being the baby for so long at home.

Ciaran had already been at school a couple of years and seemed to take everything in his stride. Ciaran and Gerald continued their school days in Warrenmount until they reached the age of seven and when they each made their First Communion they moved on to Donore Avenue Christian Brothers' School, just across the road from granny's house.

While they were there they took part in drill displays as well. Their displays were held in the grounds of Harold's Cross Dogs Race Track one year and everyone went. It was a wonderful event. They were dressed in all white and became different symmetric designs on the field in various flags formations. It was an amazing event.

Ciaran and Gerald also enjoyed singing, so they joined St. John's Lane Augustinian Church Choir and joined in the group practice singing with Brian and Terry in the back bedroom in the early hours of the weekend mornings! Those of us trying to sleep in (if that was possible) did not appreciate the early morning awakenings even if it was done in harmony!.

While Ciaran and Gerald attended their choir they thought they might like to be Altar Boys as well. They mentioned it to mammy who approached the priest in charge of Altar boys but Ciaran or Gerald didn't hear any more about it, so they weren't sure if they were refused on the grounds that their mammy and daddy just couldn't afford the surplices and cassocks, but they didn't become Altar Boys.

On one particular year there was an announcement in the paper and on radio that there would be a family fireworks display in the Phoenix Park. We were all brought for this spectacular event and we walked, walked and walked what seemed like miles and all the time Ciaran was very worried he would step in the cows doo doo's.

It appeared as though everyone was out that night walking and there was a great atmosphere with everyone cheering and sounding happy. It was pitch dark in the fifteen acres except for a few stars far above, it was also very cold but no-one minded, it was like a holiday and the display was fantastic.

After a couple of hours excitement everyone agreed it had been worth the journey. Ciaran was glad to report that everyone's shoes were muddy but no one had stepped into the cow's doo ... doos.

....

Chapter 54

Becoming a Pioneer at the age of 12

The following year I made me Confirmation with the rest of me class in the Church of St. Nicholas of Myra, Francis Street on March 30th 1955 and was patted on the cheek by the Most Rev. Dr Dunne.

Thankfully Archbishop Dunne passed me by and didn't ask me a question from the Catechism. I was feeling so nervous that I might not get the answer right.

Us newly confirmed children took the pledge and became Pioneers, promising not to let a drop of alcohol pass our lips until we reached the age of 21 years, or for life if that was possible, each of us was given a pioneer pin to display on our lapel and with the pin we were presented with a prayer card with the words of 'The Promise' which had to be said every day. We were then called by our Confirmation name: I chose Bridget.

It was an interesting occasion and I enjoyed the day in me new clothes. I wore a beret, a belted coat, a dress, gloves and knee-length stockings hand knitted by me mammy.

Some weeks before the great day it was touch and go as to whether I would be confirmed that year. I was in school and for some reason or other I couldn't hear the priest, who was visiting the Confirmation class, when he asked me a question. I could see his lips moving but no sound could I hear. I just stared at him.

The Class Sister looked cross as she waited for me to answer. She didn't realize that I couldn't hear him, I didn't know I couldn't hear him. I wasn't sure he was talking. Sister assumed I didn't know the answer. When the priest left and we were putting on our coats to go home she took me aside and gave me a note for me mammy.

I went home and gave the note to me mammy. Me mammy was cross when she read the letter but I don't know what she said to me. Mammy took off her apron and marched me to the Convent and demanded to speak to the Sister in question.

The Sister told what had happened in school but all the time me Mammy and the Sister were speaking I still couldn't hear what was being said. I didn't know I had an ear infection. I was brought to the Meath Hospital where I had me ear syringed and what I dreaded most: an injection. It seemed like life was not being fair to me - again!

At regular intervals over the years I seemed to lose me voice as well as me hearing and me mammy brought me to the Ear, Nose and Throat Hospital in Earlsfort Terrace, where I would have me throat painted with 'Magic Purple Paint' that seemed to work wonders, but I never seemed to know why it was happening to me and of course I never thought of asking, well, I was still only a child.

It was about this time also when I decided I would like to join the Girl Guides and wore the Blue uniform, taking the Guide Oath: I Promise my best, to do My Duty to God and my Country and to Obey The Guide Law. A bit like 'The Confiteor' I loved it.
There were about twenty of us who met on a Friday evening in a room at the back of the Town Hall in Rathmines, and spent a lot of time earning badges and running races. Every so often we would be taken by bus to Enniskerry, and set out to walk into Powerscourt, try our hand at lighting a camp fire after collecting twigs etc. We would sing:

'Campfire's burning, campfire's burning,
draw nearer, draw nearer,
in the gloaming, in the gloaming,
Come sing and be merry!'

On one such day, a crazy idea one of the leaders had, was to take us walking to the waterfall, so with our packs on our backs we went walking and singing:

'Swinging along the open road,
Swinging along under a sky that's clear,
swinging along the open road
All in the fall, the fall of the year.
Swinging along, swinging along,
 swinging along the open road,
all in the fall of the year.

It was not such a good idea. The leaders in charge didn't seem to realize just how far the waterfall was or how long it would take us to get there but we soon got tired.

We all arrived exhausted, our legs refusing to go any further, and we had to walk straight back to the campfire. It was getting late. We didn't even get a chance to dip our feet into the water. I can't remember if we even got a badge for effort!

I then earned a place with the Blue Guide Rangers when I was too old to be a guide. Our walking took us frequently over the Featherbeds just for fun. I just loved walking even if it was raining and cold and me feet were wet. I felt grown up belonging in the Rangers and went on to gain a few more badges to show off, now where did I put those well earned badges?

■■

Chapter 55

The Transition into Secondary

As the years went by and the all importance of a secondary education loomed ahead, I worried. The selection process took place somewhere near the end of the 6th year, when 'someone' decided who was secondary school material, or whether it would be wiser for a pupil to go into the 7th class and do Commerce for a year.

I desperately wanted to go to Secondary School, even though I knew it was going to be hard just keeping up with homework, and I wasn't very good at memorising anything very long, but somehow it was important to me at the time.

I was very pleased to learn I did get a place. I think it was something to do with someone else seeing me as 'Being Good Enough'. With a Secondary Education I felt I had a chance in life. I used to dream that I would pass the Intermediate and Leaving Certificate Exams, so I had the choice of not ending up in a factory for the rest of me life, and maybe, just maybe, I might lose me Clanbrassil Street accent.

■■■

Chapter 56

Me Wish Comes True – Sly Visits

Dressed in me Secondary uniform of navy blue and gold, even down to the school scarf and blue beret and with the big bag of books that I still wasn't big enough to carry, I proudly joined the big girls and studied, studied and studied. The classroom we moved into had bigger desks now that we were in the senior part of the school.

Outside our classroom was a life size statue of Our Lady but she didn't have any hands so one of the girls asked the Sister why Our Lady didn't have any hands and she replied, 'You girls will become Our Lady's Hands and do good works on her behalf!'.

There were breaks from studying during the school year by learning how to sew. Our first effort was hemming a cotton hankerchief followed by making a buttonhole and learning the buttonhole stitch. That year's sewing project was how to cut out and follow instructions to a paper pattern to make a slip and knickers before the school year ended. We were shown step by step how to tack up the sides, how best to thread the sewing machine needle and learn how to practice using the foot pedal to help machine up the tacked work.

Putting the elastic in the waist and knicker legs proved to be a little more difficult. The result, both articles were at least two sizes, possibly three sizes too big for me so I had to roll down the top of the knickers so I didn't end up with the elastic under me armpits, but it was a big achievement at the time!.

At cookery we learnt to bake fairy cakes, how to get the air into the mixture by stirring in a figure of eight and how to grease the baking tins to stop them from sticking, just like me mammy did. We also learnt how to make the lightest pastry by not having sweaty hands while handling it.

We learnt about weights and measures. In our laundry classes we were taught how to wash, starch a collar, do the ironing and of course clean up after ourselves. Everyone worked in pairs.

We also had singing lessons with Sr. Cecilia and became fluent in singing the Latin Mass. We also worked very hard on preparing for the Annual 'Ard Feis Coel' held in Abbey Street. Sr. Cecelia had a wonderful voice and a beautiful nature.

One of the highlights of attending Warrenmount School was being brought to St. Nicholas of Myra Church in Francis Street for Confessions one Friday in every month. During our secondary school years we were allowed to go un-escorted on the one condition that we returned to school without delay without making any detours.

To the class it was the chance of having the morning off, so we went. We all knew that a visit to St. Patrick's Cathedral which was a Church of Ireland Cathedral that if we as much as stepped inside the door, it was frowned upon by the Catholic Church and of course by our teachers in Warrenmount. They would have been horrified to hear of such a visit, and to be caught visiting such a place was practically asking to be excommunicated!. Well true to form a detour was made on our return journey to school after Confession.

I found St. Patrick's Cathedral a fascinating place to be in. It was so unlike any of the Catholic Churches and there were no Catholic Cathedrals in Dublin that looked as exciting. There were flags with different emblems hanging down from the walls just below the ceiling, down the centre of the church and non religious statues and busts along the walls including many different statues of St. Patrick. I wanted to know more every time I walked by. I felt it was a place that had to be visited regularly. St. Patrick's Cathedral seemed to call me back month after month. It wasn't just a game, but I would have been afraid to visit there on me own, I don't know why.

On one such Friday morning, even though many of the girls in the class were not parishioners of Francis Street parish, such as meself, we opted to go with the rest of the class when there wasn't a Sister with free time on her hands to watch over us. Now, in every group, organization there is always one person who just will not conform to the crowd and break the rule so on arriving back to school very late one Friday morning after another forbidden visit to St. Patrick's, in truth it was probably nearer to lunchtime, we were met by the head teacher when we walked into the class laughing. We weren't expecting anyone to be there, but we were confronted with, what was the meaning of us being so late!

Someone bravely said we had taken the long way back. The Head Sister was quite deaf and misheard what was said. Tempers did flare as she became more annoyed by the idea about us taking the route along Baggot Street, which was nowhere near Francis Street. We did try to explain it was along Clanbrassil Street we returned instead of taking the short route. We believed this all happened because one girl had returned to school early without making any detours and the rest of us arrived back a lot, lot later, saying 'There was a queue! Mea Culpa!'.

After the monthly trip to confession from school everyone was expected at Mass in Francis Street Church the following Sunday. Myra and me would always be seen there. We wore these very lovely tweed coats and hats to match that mammy had bought us. The tweed was of many different coloured threads. In those days it was compulsory for girls and women to wear hats in church and the boys and men to remove theirs in respect for God's house.

With the sun shining through the stained glass windows the rays of the sun changed the colours of our coats and hats. I just happened to be walking behind Myra and when I saw the change of colours which I thought were gorgeous, I whipped Myra's hat off and in a very loud whisper said, 'Look Myra what colour your hat is now' and there behind me was one of the Sisters from the School in the Coombe with the big white winged headress, The French Sisters of Charity Order. She grabbed the hat out of me hand, gave it back to Myra, saying something about taking off hats in church and 'See me when you get back to school on Monday'. I thanked God that day that I wasn't a pupil at her school.

During our secondary education there was a week when all girls were requested to attend the school retreat which of course was in the Winter when it was freezing cold in the mornings. Up for the seven o'clock early Mass in the Oratory every morning. It was certainly too early in the morning for us to notice an inscription made by hand while the cement was wet on a step leading up from a pathway from the Convent grounds to the Oratory are two sets of very small footprints at each side of the step and in the centre is written 'Step on the Road to Learning'.

The Retreat was a time for Short talks given by a priest or visiting nun looking for vocations and the class 'Sisters' encouraging everyone to make their Confession. In Confession according to all the girls (the same age as me) would ask the priest if it was true they could get pregnant by kissing a boy? I admit to being very naive at that time but when I used to look at the nuns I decided (for meself) that God knew they were going to be nuns so they didn't have children. He only gave babies to married people. (Now who could be that naive? You ask).

Now, Nuala, just a couple of years older than me had been already playing the 'mother role' to Rachel from the time she was born. Nuala was very serious minded, hard working and doing well in school. Everyone was sure she would be a nun some day. She went on all the retreats, she was in the Legion of Mary, she was a 'Child of Mary' at school and attended the devotions to Our Lady of the Miraculous Medal in Francis St. Church on Monday nights and went to the sodalities. Myra and me wanted to attend the devotions to our Lady of the Miraculous Medal with Nuala but our mammy said when we learnt to say the Hail Mary prayer properly, that it wasn't 'Holy Mary, Mudder eh God' all said in a rush…then maybe…I can't recall qualifying for the treat of staying up late enough to attend!.

On one of our outings to St. Stephen's Green with Nuala, Rachel was stung by a bee as they were playing on the grass. Nuala put her first aid into action by holding Rachel down on the grass and with her teeth she removed the sting. It was all over in seconds. She lifted Rachel up gave her a big hug, the tears stopped after a little while when got over the shock and Rachel smiled.

....…..........................….

Chapter 57

News

1) The August Bank Holiday of 1957 weekend brought 200,000 Irish workers with bulging wage packets back to the shores of Ireland with their families for their annual two weeks holidays with as much as £1.5m to spend.
2) Happy reunions abounded all over Ireland, with everywhere doing a roaring trade. Air Lingus had to put on extra flights for the biggest invasion ever. British Railways stood with boats at the ready and B & I Liverpool to Dublin ferries were packed. For the tourists cheap day return rail tickets were issued at all CIE Stations and direct bus services were available to connect with trains and airplanes.
3) An incident occurred that brought a crowd to the beach at Fethard Haven in Wexford that August hot day. A school of 36 killer whales swam in on the full tide getting into dangerously shallow water for their size. They missed the outgoing tide and despite all efforts of the public trying to keep them wet with buckets of sea water and using everything they had to bring them back to sea, their efforts failed and the whales died from lack of water. As whale meat is good for feeding stuffs it was sent to Ballinasloe.
4) To reassure the families of immigrants who had settled in Australia and were working in the building trade a statement was issued to all employees on City Building Projects that safety helmets were to be worn at all times and those who didn't follow this rule were liable to prosecution.
5) Around the same time The Primate of Australia, Cardinal Gilroy wrote a pastoral letter to 34 Catholic Bishops in Ireland, England and Scotland with a request that Australia needed more women immigrants. The letter read, 'We are in warm sympathy with the desire to preserve an equitable balance in our population growth by the promotion of a larger influx of Irish, English and Scotish influence upon whose cultures and traditions the Australian Commonwealth developed this portion of the Globe'.
6) On the housing front, Applicants requesting loans from Dublin Corporation under the small dwellings Acts could now do so with incomes of up to £832 a year where as previously it was only available to those on incomes of £624.
7) Recruitment began for FCA men whose training would be at Gorman's

Town Camp, Co Meath. Usually it was for a 2 week period training during the summer and then at weekends.

8) It was the year Ireland joined the International Bank and International Monetary Fund becoming the 61st member of both organizations.

9) The First TV Script to be filmed by the new Elliman-Dalton Enterprise at Ardmore Studios (Ireland) Ltd, was of the most successful play 'Twenty Years A-Wooing' at the Abbey Theatre by the new Irish playwrite and author John McCann.

10) Donegal and heather scented tweeds link Ireland with the Fashion Centres of the world. The shuttles that sing in the little town, the lonely cottages among the high hills and by the surging sea of Donegal are spinning. Irish Tweeds that are highly praised in London, New York, Paris, Rome, Hong Kong and Toronto. It is the name on everyone's lips. It is the Fashion to be seen in, a must in everyone's wardrobe. It has an artistic attractiveness and durability diversity of design in fashion houses all over the world.

11) The era of losing scarfs goes with Horst Kloess' latest design of the year 'Scarf Coat.' This new idea of a collar shaped like a scarf and knotted at the back and would look delightful is now available in Donegal Tweed!

12) This was a time when Maureen O'Hara the Irish born actress hit back at the American Magazine 'Confidential' by sueing them for $5,000,0000 (£1,785,000) when the magazine alleged she had been involved in an 'amorous scene'.

13) 'Rock 'n Roll' has arrived – and the Anti-Rock 'n Roll Movement, The Belfast Corporation Police deferred it's decision on the application for the lifting of the ban on the film 'Rock Around the Clock' with Bill Haley. It was the first Rock 'n Roll film which the Committee prohibited.

14) In the Agricultural world a new Irish invention of a turf cutting machine built by Bord Na Mona was named 'Chain Saw Bagger'

15) While the worry of TB was still in evidence and a threat to everyone, a statement by the Health Authority Radiographer who deplored indifference, appealed to the 45 year olds to become TB conscious and take advantage of the Mass X-Ray Mobile Units and make themselves available during lunch-hours. Caught in time TB could be treated and possibly save their lives.

When Terry was a little older and working, the firm who employed him in Tara Street persuaded him to attend the Mass X-Ray Mobile Unit close by. Terry was one of the lucky one's. in that he was diagnosed early because of that X-Ray and was immediately sent to Blanchardstown Hospital where he recovered with the help of the right treatment, a lot of fresh air and good food. Again he was not allowed outside contact except eye contact through a window while the disease remained contagious. He was declared safe after a year.

16) And finally, Dublin Corporation decided to provide Pedestrians Crossings for the City.
……………………………………………………………..………………....

Chapter 58

The End And A New Beginning.

Monday December 4th 1957 was to be the day when life as we knew it was to change. It was just as I was ready to leave for school when mammy called me to say she had to go out and I could stay at home to mind Rachel.

It was quite normal for me mammy to keep me off or late for school. I hated arriving late and having to give some excuse that me mammy was sick. The head sister would reply, "She looked alright last night at the Whist/Beetle Drive" There wasn't an answer for that. I was the one mammy kept late when she wanted a lend of some money from the shopkeeper down the street. But today was different I wasn't asked to run to the shop. I wasn't asked to do anything else it was just to mind Rachel.

Within a few minutes she had gone. Just before she left I asked her 'When will you be back?' and her reply was "I don't know". Rachel, our Christmas baby would be three years old on 19 December.

The morning went quickly. We stayed in, Rachel and I. I played with Rachel and she followed me around the house. We made the beds and tidied up a little. .I was hoping me mammy would be pleased.

By late morning there was still no sign of mammy returning and Aileen was due in for an early lunch. I decided I had better get something ready for Aileen to eat. Daddy had not arrived in from night work either so there was nobody there except me and Rachel.

Because Aileen worked in the bookies and the horse racing sometimes didn't start until late morning Aileen would have an early lunch. That day was no different, Brian was working in Cassidy's Drapery Shop in George's Street and Terry in Dockrell's paint shop on Tara Street, both near enough to come home for lunch, which they did, and were followed shortly afterwards by me daddy. And the next few hours were a time I never thought I would ever experience.

"Where's your mammy?" Daddy asked me.

"I don't know. She's out. She didn't say when she'd be back, she's left a letter for you on the sideboard.

Daddy went over to the sideboard where there were three letters. One with his name, one with Brian's name and one with the shop-keeper's name on it all in me mammy's handwriting.

When Daddy opened his letter time stood still. I was sitting perched on the window ledge beside the radio with Rachel on me knee and there in the kitchen was Daddy, Aileen, Brian and Terry sitting at the table with their food getting cold, even the kitchen seemed to chill and all was silent, even Rachel was quiet. Then there were tears, but nothing was being said.

Then Brian read his letter and by this time the letter to the shop-keeper had been opened also. Terry was sent out to telephone Nuala's school to tell them that she was needed at home. Everyone talked in whispers at the table, and me and Rachel sat and watched.

In one way it was like we'd been forgotten, it was as though we weren't there, but we were. It was all a haze that day, nothing seemed real. There wasn't the usual chatter among them. I sensed something was wrong rather than knew. I couldn't ever have imagined how devastating an effect this happening might have on each individual in turn .

Nuala arrived in a fluster, looking very hot and red to complete the scene. It was a scene of disbelief written all over their faces. When I saw Nuala I knew something was terribly wrong. There was more whispering and the letters were being read again and again and being passed around and everyone was trying to make sense of everything that didn't make sense. A mother just doesn't walk away, where was she? Why? Why? and Why now?

What was the most important thing to deal with, who to tell without alarming the younger children of the family who were at school? What were they going to tell Myra, Enda, Ciaran and Gerald when they came home from school, and what about the shop-keeper, who was going to explain to her there was no money. She wasn't going to get her Christmas 'Didley Money'. Our Mammy owed her a lot of money and Mammy was gone. There was no way of repaying it.

As time was getting on, they agreed the story would be that mammy had become sick and was taken to hospital and no one would be allowed to visit for a little while anyway. That was easily sorted and hopefully believable.

Then the questions were directed at me: "What was she wearing, did she have a suitcase?"

'I don't know, I was in the kitchen with Rachel when she left'

'But, what did she say to you before she left?'

'She just said she was going out and she didn't know when she would be back'. 'She told me to stay in the kitchen with Rachel so we wouldn't get cold'.

Mammy was not in the habit of kissing or hugging so me and Rachel had just waved and said goodbye as mammy left the kitchen. We only heard the front door close.

It was only later when nobody could find the nice new soft towels and face cloths they had seen mammy buy at the Christmas sale of work in Nuala's school in Kings Inn the previous Saturday that they knew mammy had planned her leaving.

Nuala's childhood had ended a long time before then but now her school days ended that day at the age of fifteen and a half. Nuala also had a Saturday job in O'Shaughneseys in Capel Street which she had to give up also. It was to be a full-time job for Nuala looking after the whole family and Daddy.

The next few days following mammy's disappearance became a nightmare. The shop keeper we knew so well and who was really a very lovely person who cared about us a great deal began to ask when she would be able to collect her savings from mammy. No one knew what to say but promised that their daddy would be down to talk to her.

He was at home meanwhile, trying to sort out how to explain there wasn't any money, not even enough to pay the weekly bill never mind the Christmas money that was owed. This was the shop keeper who had been very good to the family when the hotel strike had been on and when our daddy had been off work over Christmas that time. She had made sure we were well looked after and had put a hamper together for the family. Daddy avoided the shopkeeper until he could sort out how to explain to her what was happening at home and the problems he had himself and no money.

When he did get the courage to explain she was very understanding. That's when Daddy knew who his friends were! Those of us who knew that our mammy was gone and not likely to be coming back spent the next few years lying to everyone who asked us about our mammy. How could anyone ever admit to anyone else that their mammy had just walked out one morning and simply vanished?

Every so often the younger ones would be told by grownups outside the family, that they'd been to visit someone in the hospital where their mammy was supposed to be an in-patient, would say 'She wasn't there', no-one knew of her in the hospital'. When they asked about it at home they were told a little white lie that Mammy had been moved to another hospital. Eventually everyone was told she had been moved to a hospital in England because too many questions were being asked and there were no answers but secretly Ciaran and Gerald had worked it out for themselves.

It was a very sensitive time in our lives when we couldn't even talk about mammy in front of daddy. The subject was taboo. Whenever we tried to talk to daddy about mammy, he would say something like: "Your mother knows we still live here.

No-one could even tell their friends. Enda wanted to write to mammy and she would go on and on asking where she was living, we would try to shush her up before daddy heard her. She didn't understand - she just missed her.

Gerald recalls the time he was in school drawing his picture for the Texaco Picture Competition but didn't think his drawing was good enough but it was fun to do. He was learning to sing Jingle Bells and Silent Night for the first time. Like the rest of his class he was getting excited about Christmas coming. Then he somehow heard mammy was gone and his whole world fell apart. He saw everyone was upset and felt that everyone was in a panic.

'She can't spoil Christmas' was all he could think of.

Life returned to some normality and Nuala took mammy's place. She seemed to know what do and started preparing for Christmas herself by making the Christmas cake and Puddings and doing the shopping in Sweeneys.

....

Chapter 59

Christmas With A Difference

Christmas was almost upon us. There was no money and it seemed that everywhere daddy happened to be he would be confronted by people who said his wife owed them money, people he hadn't ever met before.

Mammy's two closest friends, Mrs. Doran and Mrs. McCullough didn't know anything about her intentions so were as shocked as daddy was about her disappearance. Daddy still refused to discuss it.

A few days before Christmas Brian and Terry set about making toys when the younger ones went to bed. Between them they made a rocking horse, possibly for Rachel? They painted it red and blue, but the paint refused to dry. The following evening one of them thought it was safe to see how strong it was, put their weight on it and it fell apart. It was too late to have it fixed for Christmas. I never found out what they ended up doing or making.

But Christmas Day did finally arrive and there was the usual excitement of exchanging presents and wanting to find our what Santa brought. After breakfast Ciaran found Santa had brought him a cowboy outfit complete with guns and holster. Gerald got an Indian suit with a beautiful head-dress of magnificent feathers but somewhere in the back of his mind he realized it wasn't new. He had seen someone else in the house wear it before, he then somehow knew there was 'No Santa', but he decided to make the best of it as he didn't think anyone else in the Lane would have a head-dress as wonderful as his.

He went off happily to play with his bow and arrow, but his happiness was short lived when he pulled back the bow too far and it broke. He was so heartbroken he ran out of the house down Clanbrassil Terrace and had the biggest tantrum of his life. That helped him sort out the big chip on his shoulder and exorcise his mammy at the same time. It was what he called a double whammy!,

After Mass and a short visit to Betty and Stella's we were invited to spend the day with the parents of Brian's fiancé, Shiela, parents who lived in Kevin Street, just down the road from Clanbrassil Street. The time spent there was thoroughly enjoyable. We enjoyed been able to watch television even if it had only a six inch screen but Mr. Scarry had placed magnifying glass over the screen to make the picture bigger for everyone to see.

Sheila's father had made the television himself at home from old radar equipment left over after the war that he had brought over from England bit by bit. They served us a very nice Christmas dinner and gave each of us a present. Sheila's mammy made us clothes and her daddy made Rachel a doll's house.

The quality of our home life improved and a sense of fairness in the house prevailed and thanks to Nuala the house was clean and each of us were allocated a weekly responsible cleaning job, including the boys. Those who were in charge of polishing the hall would put cloths on their feet and slide up and down on the hall floor to improve the shine and also their sliding techniques. The black fire-range was always gleaming. Even the family diet improved with Nuala's cooking. She introduced us to liver, even if we didn't like it. She insisted it was good for us. Nuala was a very good cook!.

Mammy's name was rarely mentioned as out of sight was indeed out of mind. There were constant visits from the police but mostly during the daytime when we were at school. It was indeed a mystery, the sudden disappearance of a mother who seemed to have vanished into thin air.

Daddy had requested that if there was any visiting being done by the Gardai could they please call when the children were at school. Unfortunately two plain clothes policeman called one morning, Myra recognized them as the Gardai and she became hysterical. She then realised what it was all about and she was very angry with everyone for not being told. Daddy was angry also because the visit had caused so much upset. The police searched the space between the backyard and the wall beyond but of course there was no trace. They seemed to forget that I had been around the morning she had left but apart from that there had been no other news and no-one had seen her since.

Myra strongly objected to Nuala being left in charge as she felt Nuala was not old enough to tell her what to do. There were times when Myra would create and threaten to run away when she was told off or asked to do something she didn't want to do. What was a threat one minute became a reality. Myra stormed out of the house slamming the front door behind her, when she wasn't back within half an hour we got a little worried, but she did come back a little calmer. Eventually we stopped worrying because we knew she had only gone down to the shop. But it did annoy Nuala who then told Myra that when she was thinking of running away, could she please run away on the nights that daddy was at home!.

One very nice sunny day during the summer school holidays after mammy left, Myra and her friend Clare Doherty decided to go to Bohernabreena to pick blackberries. Myra didn't have a bike but Clare did so Myra borrowed a bicycle with faulty brakes, or possibly it didn't have any brakes! They had a lovely time until the return journey home. As they cycled fast down a steep hill Myra's bike went out of control. She only vaguely remembered the police and going home in a police car. Nuala and her friend Frances were at home when the police knocked on the door to leave Myra in Nuala's care.

Everyone thought Myra was OK even Myra thought she was OK until, she started saying things like, 'Frances is me best friend!' and other silly things. Nuala got a bit worried and took her to the Meath Hospital to have her checked over. Myra was kept in for a week, although to all intents and purposes, it appeared as though she was fine the following morning.

Being an inpatient was quite an experience for Myra because it was the first time that she'd ever been fussed over by adults. She was one of two children in that part of the hospital and the adults shared their fruit and books with her. She was very sad to leave the hospital and come home to 100 Lower Clanbrassil Street.

....

Chapter 60

Daddy

Our Daddy was a small man with a big sense of humour and a generous heart. Somehow I used to think he thought he and his family were well off. Every so often he would give the kitchen furniture away to the St. Vincent de Paul Society, and then buy new furniture from Cavendish's Furniture Shop in North Great Georges Street and pay for it weekly, on Hire Purchase otherwise known as on 'The Never, Never'.

Sometimes he even gave away some of our clothes when we were out. Now, none of use really ever knew why? We had very few clothes to call our own. I was missing one very treasured emerald green dress with a little black velvet bow, it just vanished, ne'r to be seen again … well not in our house.

We possessed one tallboy and one wardrobe between us in our bedroom. Clothes just didn't get lost easily. I pined for that dress for a very long time, it even invaded my dreams. All I could hope was, that the new owner appreciated it!

Our Daddy always worked in a hotel. He cycled there and back every night and every morning and mostly everywhere else. It was the only form of transport in our house while we were still young and at school.

Our Daddy had a sense of humour so on one occasion when we were all sitting at home one evening doing our homework in the kitchen we heard the front door being slammed back to the wall. we all looked at each other, nobody moved and there wasn't a sound from us, we just waited and we heard daddy's bike banging off the wall in the hall and then along the scullery. Then the kitchen door opened and there was daddy with what looked like a big red cut across his forehead and down his cheek and a handkerchief in his hand, looking as though he was about to collapse

We were dumb-struck and horrified, but then the red strip off his cigarette packet started lifting away from his face. 'Fooled you', says he. We all broke into hysterical laughter.

Our daddy was liked by everyone and he was always called by his Christian name, Leo.

On the nights our daddy was working this was the routine. Someone would bring him up his tea and the evening newspaper on a tray while he was still in bed, if for any reason our daddy was lavish with his money before he went to bed in the morning, the advice to us all was 'Don't spend the money' as daddy would have remembered he'd given his money to someone, couldn't remember who but was also likely to ask for it back.

Shortly after finishing his tea daddy would come down stairs to shave at the kitchen table. There in front of him was laid out on a newspaper at the end of the table, was, a basin of hot water, his razor, shaving stick, shaving brush, face cloth, soap on a saucer and a towel on his knees to stop the drips from his razor getting on to his trousers, and a jar of Brylcream for his hair. After his shave and washing his face and neck there would be the usual cry:

"Now where are me back and front studs? Anyone seen me cufflinks? You can never find anything is this house!, who'se moved me clean collar? Did anyone collect me clean starched collars from the laundry? Can someone run across the road to 'Somers' for a front stud?' Our Daddy was waited on hand and foot like he was the king! And we guessed he was.

On our Daddy's two nights off he would take his turn washing the delph with his shirt sleeves rolled up. He would lay out newspaper on the kitchen table and a basin of hot water. After he washed each piece of delph he would lay it on the newspaper to drain making rivers of water in the newspaper and bubbles soaking through until someone dried the delph.

Also on those nights when mammy and daddy got dressed up and went out, Brian was left 'children minding' he would bring one or two friends in and they would play games with us and play jokes on us.

One expression I used to hate when they were playing cards with us when Brian or Terry would put the 'Whammy' on me and because I would get so angry and had little or no sense of humour, they enjoyed it more and I always lost! Who needed brothers? I thought they were shocking mean.

Another game Brian and his friends would play on us was: We can lift you to the ceiling. They would send us out into the hall and tell us to come in one at a time. As we entered the kitchen they would blindfold us, we were then put sitting on a plank of wood and they would lift the plank a few inches, tap us with a book on the head and say "You've just hit the ceiling".

Now who would disbelieve them?

There were many other tricks they played on us much younger and much more innocent brothers and sisters, on our Daddy's nights off.

Chapter 61

Betty and Stella

During our many visits to O'Donovan Road as we got older we noticed things more and became aware of what adults did that we weren't allowed to do or didn't know how to do, we watched as Stella and Betty improved their technique of smoking and me and Myra copied in mime.

I even tried it in our back yard once with a sheet of rolled up newspaper, lit it, inhaled, practically choked meself and was lucky I didn't set me hair on fire! Not to be tried again!

Betty and Stella smoked but Evelyn didn't and Aileen started smoking as well. It was the grown up thing to do. It was like everyone we met seemed to smoke so we didn't think about it. Our daddy and uncle Pearse smoked as well! We came from a family of smokers.

Our aunties seemed rich in our eyes and we also thought our aunts were very lucky. They lived in a house that had a kitchen where the cooking was done, and there was a dining room that was off their kitchen which had an open marble fireplace with a mantelpiece over it where souvenirs and postcards from their holidays were kept. In front of the blazing fire were placed two armchairs.

We would all try to sit on the same armchair to watch the flames in silence as granny was always resting in the other armchair. We only had a range in our kitchen and even the front of it had a door over the bars, so we couldn't see much there. There was an open fireplace in our parlour but that was only used for Christmas and maybe for visitors.

An open fireplace with flames licking around the wood, turf, brickettes or coal, brought imaginary pictures to life and being allowed to sit that close was a special treat. Hung on the wall over the fireplace were three flying ceramic birds of different sizes and somewhere in the house they had a weather clock that they had brought back from one of their holidays.

Sometimes the conversation would take in the weather, "Is it going to rain today?" and Stella or Betty would say: "Let's have a look at the weather clock, Is the lady standing outside with her umbrella or does the man have his sunglasses on?" or maybe it was the other way around.

Betty and Stella could also afford to go on holidays with their friend

Patsy, Rita and sometimes with Pearse and Doris to such places as Italy, Germany, France and Spain and bring back souvenirs and practice their new acquired foreign languages. We all learnt how to say 'Thank You' and 'You're Welcome' in four languages. What four languages you ask? Grazi, Prago (Italian), Danke, Bitte (German), Por Favor, Gracias (Spanish) and we all learnt French in School and of course Gaeilge. But they would tell us all about the exciting things they saw and did and of course showed us all the photos Stella loved to take with her Kodac Brownie camera.

Chapter 62

Why Don't You Leave Me Alone?

When I was about fifteen years old an unexpected appointment from a portacabin clinic located on Nicholas Street arrived for me to attend to have blood tests. That went all right until a follow-up appointment was received for me to attend St. Vincent's Hospital which was situated on St. Stephen's Green.

I had been about eight years old when mammy had stopped bringing me to Harcourt Street Children's hospital and I had begun to believe that I was cured of whatever it was they were treating me for. I was eating what everyone else was eating and although I knew I got tired easily that was it. Now it was happening again, why couldn't they leave me alone?

Was I to be hounded every few years. I had no real complaints. Yes, I was still small for me age but I wasn't often sick or complaining, so why now?

On the way to St. Vincent's, Nuala had drilled me on what I was supposed to say about me diet and all the good foods I was eating. I forgot to tell them that Nuala was feeding me and the rest of the family such foods as liver and kidneys, mince meat with lots of onions, carrots and gravy and potatoes, and gigot chops and a lot more besides.

I let Nuala down badly, because I still had that fear of doctors and hospitals. I was just dumb-struck: I couldn't think of a thing to say but I couldn't take me eyes off the doctor for one second. I was never sure what they might do to me even now when I was in me teens but still at school.

The whole purpose of the appointment was the question. Was I menstruating? The answer was 'No'. The medical professionals believed Coeliac Disease possibly slowed down the process in the child and they wanted to do more tests. I was to be admitted when a bed became available.

The bottom fell out of me world. There was no way I was going into hospital. The dread hung around me for what seemed like months. Apparently even then there seemed to be a bed shortage. However, as I was getting ready to go swimming after school a few months later during those months of worry I discovered I was menstruating and that was the end of me problems.

      The hospital was contacted and I was discharged. I was allowed to continue with me ordinary life with no mentions of special diets or you can't eat this or you can't eat that. I weighed six stone and my height was four feet and eleven inches. All of a sudden life was wonderful. I was not living in the shadow of hospitals. I was being the average teenager and I didn't mind not being allowed to go swimming that day!

••

Chapter 63

More Thoughtful

Daddy seemed to care more about what was happening at home and was more visible to us than he had been previously and he was reminded by Nuala of everything that was needed for the house and by the rest of the family.

He tried to make life easier for Nuala by buying a Twin-Tub washing machine to help with the washing and he bought a Tintawn carpet for the kitchen floor to help keep the heat in. He would also buy Nuala a present of a box of chocolates now and again.

Those of us who were still at school looked a lot cleaner and tidier as well. Unfortunately for the rest of us who were younger, as well as daddy to answer to, we also had Brian, Terry, and Nuala to answer to, and Aileen when she was there.

Terry was a bit of a bossy boots at home. With black hair, very dark brown eyes and bushy eyebrows his looks belied him giving the impression to all and sunder outside, of him being shy, he wasn't. He loved the theatre, took up drama and played some small parts in some of the Operas and had a small part in the pantomimes held in the Gaeity and the Olympia Theatres.

He frightened the life out of me on the street one afternoon. I was casually walking along New Street looking into shop windows and every time I stopped the sound of footsteps behind me stopped. I walked on, the footsteps followed. I was afraid to look around. I quickened me pace. The footsteps quickened. I was panicking inside and then Terry walked past me with a grin on his face!. I could have happily murdered him on the spot.

While the drama of me mammy was unfolding in our household in Clanbrassil Street our Granny was giving support and advice to Daddy. Betty and Stella were doing a great deal of knitting for us and making sure they were there for us if we needed them. They were being responsible for some of our needs and they did their best.

Not much went un-noticed by our granny. I only ever remembered me Granny being old. She always wore black and had snow-white hair. When she'd fall asleep in her armchair beside the fire, which she did quite often, her mouth drooped at the corners while she relaxed. I was fascinated with that expression and would imitate her as she slept.

When Myra and me were in our teens we would spend alternative Saturday afternoons with our granny to keep her company. Betty and Stella would come in for their early lunch of tripe cooked in milk with carrots, onions and potatoes, it looked just like a lamb's wooly coat, but was the stomach of a bullock, (not something I needed to know at the time). Tripe was an acquired taste and Granny wouldn't take 'I don't like that' from anyone so everyone acquired a taste for it because it was served up every Saturday.

When Betty and Stella went back to work after their dinner granny would insist I had an hour's rest with her on her very high bed, well it seemed high to me! Me granny would fall asleep snoring with her mouth open but teenage girls do not sleep in the afternoon so it was just a question of how long would the 'rest' be before it was time to go out?.

Finally rested and ready for a slow walk to the South Circular Road where we would catch a bus going to Whitefriar Street Church for confessions, in Angier Street. If the conductor on the bus didn't ask for the fare and I didn't force it on him, I would find meself being practically sent running after the bus to pay him, because it was a SIN. So there was no keeping the bus fare, not then anyway!

After confessions and lighting a few candles, one for ... and one for ... we would then slowly walk down George's Street to Cassidy's clothes shop, that good quality shop where me granny would buy knickers and nylons for herself and a pair of knickers for me.

Now and again she would also buy me a hanky as it appeared I seemed to have a constant sniff anytime I was with me granny. I relied on me sleeve just like everyone else did!. Anyway even if me granny did buy me a hankie I never seemed to have it with me when I was visiting her. Maybe I only had a sniff when I visited without the hankie ... well who knows ...

■■

Chapter 64

How Do I Feel?

Back at school I wondered if the nuns knew about the situation at home and it became evident that they did. They were sympathetic knowing I had been the one left minding me baby sister when me mammy had left. I felt they were being extremely lenient with me when I was not producing the work I was supposed to be doing, but I was still trying. Me mind was constantly wandering off. I wasn't sure how I was supposed to feel about me mammy going away. I didn't think I liked me mammy before she left but I was now feeling very mixed up. Was it alright to feel glad that she was gone?

Up late every night, then up early every school day studying just to keep up and some days it felt like I'd never even opened a book in me life. Me mind would go blank. It was proving a tough challenge. I was doing me best but sometimes it felt as though it wasn't enough. I was losing the battle.

The class was very competitive. There was a girl sitting beside me who had her hand up for everything. She had all the answers and the mathematic problems worked out before me and most of the girls in the class had walked up the school slope that morning. I could have nudged her for ever for a prompt but she wouldn't give in. She was good at everything and had only joined the class for her Secondary. Education

I really did work hard at keeping up with the class for the second year of secondary but the reports were not as positive as I needed them to be to keep striving for that ultimate prize of achievement, The Intermediate Certificate. Always the same report: 'Doing well, Could do better!' not really the great incentive to keep trying. It didn't do anything for me morale. How many hours were there in the day and when was I supposed to sleep?

Success! I had passed the end of year exams. I was still holding me own, or just about, but I still needed someone to believe in me.

During that summer holiday break from school with only one year to go before the final exam for the Intermediate Certificate I took me first summer job. I didn't know then that I would not be going back to Warrenmount School or that I wouldn't sit for that much coveted prize The

Intermediate Certificate. I was finished with school as I knew it then.

But, I couldn't leave it there, I began to take on night classes in Crumlin Road Technical School year after year. First it was a course in tailoring, (dressmaking), where I made me first blouse and it fitted me. The following year a Shorthand and Typing course with a teacher who had taught me in school. The teacher wore the same grey two piece suite with a white blouse to the class every week and black high-heel shoes with seamed nylons that looked very smooth on her. We got on well together. I did enjoy wanting to learn, but on my terms.

••

Chapter 65

Earning Money!

I began me working life in a factory making zips!. Not the rosy future career I had planned when I started at secondary school, but I had taken the first job that came along on the first week of the school summer holidays. I had intended going back to school but it turned out to be much more fun not having to worry about school and memorizing lessons.

The factory, 'Wings Zipmakers' was just a big room next door to Hector Grey's toy shop in Liffey Street. It was certainly the beginning of a wider education for me: I had entered the world of swearing and of hearing dirty jokes. I was mixing with people who hadn't gone to Warrenmount school and hadn't had elocution lessons.

I was rubbing shoulders with everyone on the working bench. We learnt about measuring, fixing, remaking, sorting and choosing colours, fixing nickel zip teeth and putting ends and stoppers on zips. We were like a big gang of friends and had lots of laughs and no worries.

It was an extremely boring job but everyone got paid and that was the big bonus, money, money, money, not a great deal of it but enough to give Nuala some for housekeeping. When the summer holidays ended Nuala had the job of telling the head sister in Warrenmount I wasn't returning to school.

After a year in Liffey Street the owners of 'Wing's Zipmakers' decided to expand and moved everyone and everything to a laneway in Rathmines. It was to premises next door to the Tayto factory where they made the famous Tayto Crisps. The whole place smelt of cooking oil and the girls who worked there had their hair in rollers under their hairnets and white hats, to keep their hair from catching fire. Their aprons didn't look too clean either, but the crisps were tasty. The smell of the crisps wafted into our Zip Factory.

'Wings' factory was behind the Town Hall. It was a much bigger place than the place in Liffey Street and in a quieter area away from busy roads and traffic. A weaving department, a new addition to the factory that hadn't been part of the factory in Liffey Street was now added, as well as the machinery for making the zip teeth was situated upstairs. There was an assembling bench with more elaborate machinery for re-enforcing the ends of the zips and a lot of acetate and heat used in the assembling. We became experts at assembling from scratch but it was a very noisy place when all the machinery was working. Downstairs was the paint shop where the zips material was sprayed transforming them into a rainbow of colours. Three of me new friends, Teresa, John and Kathleen worked in the paint shop and I could name all the new introduced colours just by looking at their working house coats which were supposed to be blue but were more than that.

I worked on the assembly line upstairs where the music blared overhead and we sang along to all the new record songs played on the radio and everyone talked about their latest boyfriend and the best place to go dancing. One of the girls called Connie was into ballroom dancing so the point of conversation always got around to ballroom dresses and clothes for dancing.

Connie lived in Cabra. Teresa, blond, beautiful, and with a set of perfectly straight white teeth, and me, became great friends. We went dancing together and followed the latest pop-idols antics. Wing's was also where I had me first crush on Sean, one of me bosses. He was a lot older than me, he was married and probably didn't even remember me when I left. I didn't think anyone knew about 'me crush on him', but they did. All I could do was dream about him and watch his every move. I lived in hope of being noticed! I could have been accused of stalking at the time but it was only a girlie thing!.

Because I was the newest member of staff and of course there wasn't a fully fitted staffroom with tea making facilities or anything fancy, just a kettle, a teapot, a bag of Lyons Tea-leaves, a bag of sugar, enough cups and spoons to go around and a sink to wash up the cups and spoons in. I became the messenger and had to do the running to the shop around the corner, for the staff. Everyday I was given a list of things to buy, e.g. 3 club milks, 4 packets of Silvermints, 2 iced sponge squares, 2 bottles of milk etc. and that was ok except in the winter months when even the workplace was not overly warm and I'd rather not go out, but looking on the bright side of things, the daily outing to the shop broke up the morning.

In the midst of all the swearing, the rude jokes and the messing about there were two sisters who spent their time telling everyone off and encouraging us to do a retreat in the Marie Reparatrix Convent near Mount Street. Amazingly, a few of us went.

It was doubtful that any of us were used to a cushioned life but we found the benches in the church were very hard and our concentration very poor. I was fascinated with how still the Sisters knelt for such a long time, but that didn't improve my kneeling or sitting, quietly.

Because I had to walk to Rathmines every morning and back home in the evening five days a week to work I decided it was time to buy a second hand bicycle. It was a very big decision for me even though I was sixteen, to even think about riding a bicycle. I'd always had a secret desire to ride a bicycle but when I was very young I tried riding a three wheeler bicycle, that didn't belong to me, down the Lane footpath and both bike and me went straight into a garden wall and railing. That time I ended up with a bleeding nose but felt lucky it wasn't a broken nose. Later on I tried riding a 2 wheeler scooter and even that wouldn't go straight. I think I must have had me eyes closed in fear!

I wasn't very good with speed either: I steered clear of anything that might sweep me away. But most of me friends could cycle and I felt I was losing out without one. So by the time I had started working and I could afford a grown up ladies bike, it became the love of me life.

When I took me first journey on me bike, the saddle was just a fraction too high and I was feeling very nervous. I was on me own at twenty minutes past eight on a winter's morning. There was no way I was going to sit on the saddle just in case I couldn't get off it if I needed to. Just as well, the milk float in front of me, I knew the milk-float ran on electricity and that it couldn't have been going that fast but it made an emergency stop! But it was OK. I felt I was in control of the brakes. It was actually quite a long time before I could allow meself sit on the saddle, even though me legs were awfully tired resting on the pedals!.

Me, Nuala, Myra and
Our little sister
Rachel

Aileen's Wedding – We were there,
L-R Me, Enda, Auntie Stella, Doris, Pearse and their daughter Adele,
Auntie Evelyn and Rachel in front of Auntie Stella.

1959 Me with me friends John Greenfab and Theresa Moran on me left side. with Kathleen Smith on me right, sitting on the boss' VW.

All dressed up for me brother Terry's wedding in Manchester 1964

Chapter 66

Let's Dance!

I had now reached the age where I was feeling grownup and bringing in a wage, small though it was. It was also a time for discovering the best places to go dancing and where the best bands were playing.

Great places like the YMCA on the South Circular Road (later to be named The Garda Club) where me and Teresa went Wednesdays and Saturday for jiving and smooching and spent many happy hours dancing to the sounds of Joe Dolan and the Drifters, Dickie Rock and the Miami Show Band, and the current bands playing 'In The Mood'. There was only a Soft Drinks Bar in the dance halls then. For 'dutch courage' some of the lads went for a drink before they arrived.

People would arrive in groups and the doorman would look suspiciously at anyone who arrived on their own. The girls held up the walls on one side of the dance hall while the boys huddled around in safety numbers on the opposite side, most of them smoking. Everyone eyeing up each other looking but not looking and trying to muster up dutch courage to ask someone to dance and hoping they wouldn't be refused or left on their own when everyone else was dancing.

Within a little while, people had paired up or exchanged partners. There was the jive, the twist and the fox-trot. When looking for variety of dancehalls and becoming followers of the latest dance bands and to meet different people, Dublin had its fair share of places: The Chrystal; the 4 Provinces; The Ierne; The Irish Club in Parnel Square, where there were people at the side of the floor ready to break in and separate them if the couples were dancing too close, The Olympic (for over 18s only), The CIE, The Garda Siochana Hall in Kevin Street, The National and the Jewish Hall on the South Circular. Road. I once even ventured up to the Ritz in Ballyfermot where Theresa lived. It was very lively and as usual crowded and the lights were down low just like everyone wanted.

It was the era of Cliff Richard, Elvis Presley, Pat Boone, Chubby Checker, Billy Fury and the Blockettes, Buddy Holly and the Crickets, Jerry Lewis, a whole lot of shaking going on, Roger Whittiker, Guy Mitchell, Gerry and the Pacemakers, Chuck Berry, Brenda Lee, Bill Haley and many others.

Oh Yes, Adam Faith who sang 'What Do You Want, If You Don't Want Money ...' I liked him! Me and a few friends went to see Adam Faith on Stage at the Capital and the screams were deafening, we couldn't hear him at all. When there was a lull in the screaming, we started screaming ourselves just to show how annoying it was. We nearly got beaten up!

I bought the New Musical Express paper to keep up with the words of the latest pop songs. At the same time I would spend time before going to bed doing some stretching exercises. I'd hold on to the end of the iron bed frame in our bedroom and the bed beside it and balance me self on me toes stretching as far back as possible and even by holding the frame at the top of the bed and stretching me legs to touch the other bar at the end of the bed in the hope of becoming taller. It didn't work, but I kept trying. I drank PLJ to lose weight, as I was still small and chubby, not the best measurements to get a fella when me friend Theresa was such a blond bombshell

With Theresa being me friend she showed me a world so different and more challenging than I'd ever known before. She introduced me to roller skating at The Rink, in Angier Street. It was an amazing place with people skating around and around to the blaring music and the screeching and laughing of everyone having fun.

I had no co-ordination, I couldn't keep me feet parallel, they were all over the place even with people holding each of me arms pulling me along. I was nearly doing the splits! I loved the atmosphere, never really learnt to roller skate on me own but learnt to sit on the sideline and watch, the company was great and all Theresa's friends were friendly and didn't mind who was who's friend.

I also found I was great at knitting and could follow a pattern. I knit chunky jumpers for me self because they didn't take too long to knit and I knitted a chunky red and white jumper to wear to the 'the Rink' so I'd be recognized and remembered. Myra just happened to borrow that particular jumper (and she wasn't supposed to!) and I didn't know then. It was only when we were standing at our front door talking to friends one evening and someone called out to Myra, 'I saw you at the Rink last week!' I could feel a row coming on!

Sometimes me and me friend Maura Smith (from down the Lane) would eat ice-cream and listen to the juke box in the Ice Cream Parlour named Caffolas in the Rainbow on O'Connell Street with it's symbol of the rainbow over the door. We loved being seen there. It was the only place to be. It had a great atmosphere and it was where the young people hung out.

We were served at our table, no standing around for us, We had money, that magic word 'Money' brought visions and dreams of what we never had or ever likely to have in the near future. It was not a lot but enough to get us two scoops each of our favourite flavours of ice cream. That's what we had every visit: 2 scoops of ice cream in a dish. We couldn't afford the banana boat dish but a stainless steel dish that made a terrible screeching noise when the last and best bit of the ice cream had melted at the bottom of the dish was being scraped off, short of licking the dish, it was delicious and tasted like more.

There was never any hurrying us out of the parlour so we stayed there listening to the jukebox that was continually playing. We could even select our very own songs as there was a program setter at each table. We put our hard earned money in the slot and chose the song number we wanted to hear again and again and chatted about boys, clothes, records and who was going out with who?

Hairdressers did a great trade as it was the era of perms and curls, chemists sales boomed as young teenagers bought rollers and clips for their hair and another generation were ready to explore with make-up and hairsprays

Chapter 67

Freedom

Having a bicycle was having freedom of the city, the seaside and the countryside. If you didn't mind being saddle-sore and had staying power, it was the freedom of the world as well. Maybe not, but at least Dublin was our Oyster.

There was very heavy traffic even then in Dublin with hundreds of bikes plying for space on the roads, travelling back and forth to work. Cyclists would inch out to the front of the traffic stopped at traffic lights and when the lights changed, they were off as though it was the 'Tour De Dublin.'

Many bikes were bought and many of them stolen. One of them happened to be Myra's - her new bike. She'd loaned it to me for work when mine had a puncture. I did lock it, I swear I did, in the bicycle shed, I worked late that evening but when I came out, it was gone.

One of me many nightmares was what was I going to tell Myra?. I even had to borrow money to get home!

I loved cycling to Blackrock and Seapoint in the summer evenings. It was such a pleasure and it was a straight run, about six miles. Along the way there was the usual musical merry go-round with the hobby-horses going up and down. The swings would go higher and higher as the kids and grown-ups would squeal and scream with delight.

I would stop for an ice cream or some candy-floss that just melted in me mouth. If I was early enough I would catch the few remaining songs being played by a brass band further up the coast.

I only once ventured to Bray and back on the bicycle with Ciaran when we did a Charity Ride. It was a very tough ride on an extremely wet Sunday. The morning started off nice enough but when the rain started everyone taking part got soaked to the skin. The sun would come out and dry us off but then it rained on and off all day. It was me first experience of finding out how long it takes to cycle twenty miles, it takes forever!

By the time we arrived back, the blue, green and black diamond chunky jumper I'd knitted which fit me to me waist when I started out that morning, soaked up so much rain it was like a coat that ended down to me knees. Some boys were laughing at me because they thought I wasn't wearing anything else. Ciaran threatened to beat them up if they didn't stop. My hero!.

When I became more adapt at cycling and no longer in fear of the Dublin city roads, two friends, Theresa Taylor, whom I'd met at Warrenmount Club and Teresa Moran whom I'd met up with from me first job in the famous 'Wings', would meet some Sunday afternoons when the weather was fine and cycle to Portmarnock beach, that was quite a route and a lot of it was off the coast road.

If you liked sand, sand and more sand then Portmarnock was the place to be. It was a beach where the donkeys were brought out to give rides to young children along the sand and it was where a pot of tea could be bought and carried in a basket with the cups and spoon.

Tea always tasted better on the beach in the fresh air. There me and me friends would meet up with some young-fellas and roll around the sand-dunes for a kiss and a cuddle and possible a swim in the sea, all very innocent at the time. On occasions we would stop off at Dollymount where we would cycle across the wooden bridge making sure our wheels didn't get caught between the wooden planks.

Like the tide at Sandymount we would often find we needed to get off and walk quite a distance to find the water deep enough to swim but we weren't in any great hurry so it didn't matter.

Fairview park was the place to be on Sunday mornings if you were into football. All the friendly matches were played there and each player could be seen sporting the colours of their own school or club.

On Sunday evenings Fairview Park during the summer was a place where there was an open-air ceili of music and dancing and people came from around the area just to be part of it. There were a few lights on the nearby trees and the music could be heard from the road. We all thoroughly enjoyed being part of it so we'd lock up the bikes, mingle with the young crowds, muscle in on the dancing and if we were lucky, meet boys and have some craic.

The main aim of these activities was of course to be with the fellas. Then we would cycle home across town before it got too late, as I had to be home before 11 o'clock or God help me. Brian was in charge and would come close to the front door when it came near to the magic hour.

The usual question 'Who were you with?' On one occasion me and me friends heard there was a ceili being held off Berkley Road so three of us went. We did enjoy the evening, but not many people turned up so we separated from the boys and cycled off together down the North Circular Road only to end up with Theresa and me bicycle handle bars getting caught up together and the two of us landing on the road with a buckled wheel and bent handle-bars.

Lucky for us it was a quiet evening on the road. We were outside the Mater Hospital but we had no intentions of spending our evening in the Accident and Emergency Department so we bought some plasters from a corner shop, patched up our minor injuries and walked our bikes on the pavement through town down O'Connell Street, past the Gresham, over the Liffey Bridge, past the Bank of Ireland up Dame Street and the rest is a blur as along the way we met some very handsome young teenagers down from Offaly for the match. They did offer to wheel our bicycles for us but we didn't trust them just in case they were thinking of pinching them: well we'd only just met them!

The four of us walked as far as Theresa's granny's house off Kevin Street and then me new boyfriend walked me and me bike home to Clanbrassil Street. It was only 10.30pm and the dead-line was 11pm so we had time to get to know each other's kisses and the possible future dates we might have.

As with all good things, it ended at 11pm and we never met again, but it was good while it lasted, shame was I could never remember his name, but then again maybe it was just as well.

Palmerston Park was another place to find enjoyment. It was easy to get to on a number 12 bus and not too far beyond Rathmines. It was the nearest place that could be described as a wood. It was quite dense with trees and in the middle was a clearing with fallen trees and logs that could be climbed or scramble about on.

I just loved the smell of the damp earth and bracken and it made me feel good and left me with a sense of freedom. Another place we discovered while out cycling was Herbert Park where the tennis courts looked inviting. We thought it was a great place to spend an afternoon.

With our newly acquired expert sewing experience gained at Our Lady's Club we were able to make our own tennis mini-skirts. We weren't any good at playing tennis but we were full of enthusiasm. We could only imagine what we would do if only we'd had money.

October 1958 was a month of sadness and then rejoicing. It was a very sad day for the Catholic Church all over the world when on the 9th October 1958 Eugene Pacelli, Pope Pius X11 died after suffering a stroke.

Everywhere in the Dublin streets the Papal Flags were flying at half-mast over buildings and the public everywhere were sporting purple and yellow ribbons on their lapel.

After the conclave in Rome, Angelo Guiseppe Roncalli on the twelfth ballot was elected as the new Head of the Catholic Church and chose the title John XX111. October 28 was a day of prayer and thanksgiving when the new Pope was crowned with a silver and gold Tiara adorned with three crowns.

On his first day Pope John XX111 made a plea for World Peace.

Nuala and me were out doing parish visiting in the vicinity of the Liberties on behalf of the Legion of Mary. I was new to the Legion of Mary and joined Nuala in Meath Street Parish Hall. One of the little worries I experienced was not having money to put into the secret collection, but I somehow seemed to have loose buttons in me pocket and the chance of one of them being found in the collection purse was a constant worry!

■■'

Chapter 69

Joining A Club!

Because young people were then allowed to leave school at fourteen years old and were eager to go out to work and earn some money for their keep Sister Anthony and four past pupils of Warrenmount School, saw the need for a Girls Club, for those who had left school and now had time on their hands in the evenings.

Many could also do with a little help in making clothes for themselves, meet new friends, learn some cooking and some play-acting or make things for the Sales of Work. It was considered such a great idea that a little later they were joined by Sr. Margaret Mary. I joined a few months after I left school. I made lots of friends who became important in me life over the next few years.

The club was well attended and was fun to be part of. Sr. Anthony encouraged us girls to join in all the cookery competitions held every year by the Dublin Gas Board in D'Olier Street – our famous rock cakes were a regular.

Me friend Noeleen swapped some of her cakes with my cakes because hers looked better than mine, so with some of hers and some of mine on both plates, we both won a prize!. We were sure Sr. Anthony or Sr. Margaret Mary would not have approved.

In the Annual Dressmaking Competition held by the Singer Sewing Machine Company, Dublin, many of us learnt how to sew and we did very well, with Sr. Anthony's help. We had to make something to wear and model it. It was me first experience of the cat-walk but it was great fun. Surprisingly I didn't feel nervous: I just enjoyed the experience. I won two prizes, a sewing kit and a voucher. I felt like I was walking on air all the way home afterwards.

Sr. Anthony only saw the positive side of everyone's full potential and she was good at sharing a joke or two with us. One of the girls used to call her 'Sr. Pal'.

The girls didn't have to take part in any activity if they didn't want to. Some of them only attended because they loved the company and would just sit and chat all evening.

Sr. Anthony and the club leaders even helped to put on plays in the school hall and for those of us who were never 'Stars' at school we certainly were when taking part in the club concerts and we loved it. We danced the Tarantella and the Waltz and every time I hear those pieces of music, it takes me back to that stage and that year.

One year I played the part of the Hangman in one of the historic plays. The thing I was most embarrassed about was having to wear long black knickers to mid-thigh and black tights. I had to wear a hangman's hood to cover me identify. Oh, I did want to be recognized but not in that rig-out!

During the club parties at Christmas there was many a song we sang but our favorite was:

'One finger, one thumb keep moving,
one finger and thumb keep moving,
one finger and thumb keep moving
we'll all be merry and bright,

And after that we would add, an arm, a leg, a nod on the head, stand up, sit down, keeping moving, etc. etc. we'll all be merry and bright?'

I have a feeling Nuala's friend Olive, taught us that song. It was always a great laugh! Nuala and Olive came to all the stage events and were very supportive.

There were also many outings to the seaside and we would bring the club portable record player with a selection of 45's records and the music would be played at full blast but because it was open air with the sound of the sea in the background, it really didn't disturb too many. We would all dance and sing and we could be as noisy as we liked and mess about without being in trouble as long as we were within view of the Club Leaders.

For one weekend only it was arranged for everyone to stay in a house in Wicklow. There was a crowd of us from aged fifteen upwards and we travelled by coach. OK, we did have Sr. Anthony, Sr. Margaret Mary and the four club leaders to keep us in tow.

It was a truly amazing house. We looked at it with awe as we traveled up the gravel Avenue between trees so tall and stately and thick with leaf, with the sunlight drifting through, it was a vision from another world. It's vastness a size unseen by many of us before. It's grey stone with ivy clinging to the walls and around the windows.

It was definitely a Mansion in our eyes. We explored and ran our hands over the glass and along the window panes and glanced at the view outside, blue skies and green fields. It was a vision beyond belief, a haven in the countryside, this mansion with a portal door and pillars on both sides.

The hall itself echoed of voices past but the décor didn't, it had not been occupied by a family recently but had become a weekend self-catering hostel for groups. Apart from the bedrooms upstairs all activities happened downstairs.

The floors were covered in linoleum but we were used to that but the kitchen adjoining the house had a stone floor and an earthenware square sink with of course only cold running water, just like home so I guessed we weren't going to be any more comfort wise in the countryside than we were in the city!

We slaved for the first couple of hours carrying the heavy boxes from the coach to the house and emptying the boxes of food and luggage and finding places to put them.

We were given blankets and sheets and half listened to the rules of the do's and don'ts of the house. We shared the chores, peeling potatoes, scraping the vegetables, cooking and cleaning and it was much more fun doing it together. Well we had to eat, didn't we? We also had to make up the bunk beds for later.

We played our records in the evenings with all the windows open and danced, told stories, entertained and sang along with pop songs being played with words that we'd learnt off by heart. This went on until the club leaders wanted some peace and quiet. We were sent upstairs where the bunk beds were all together in a row so a lot of climbing was done before each one was claimed. But, beds were not for sleeping in, but for laughing and messing about until sleep took over in the early hours of the morning.

During the day time we went on long walks along the country lanes. Girl guide songs were resurrected and sung with gusto, our hair damp and flowing, our bodies free of city and traffic pollution. Someone tried to teach us the names of the trees and flowers along the way.

The weekend hours were filled with spontaneity and youthfulness and an eagerness to remain in that moment, in that time and place. It was a sad day when the weekend ended and everything was packed again for the journey back to Dublin.

....

Chapter 70

Our First Wedding Invitation – Our Only Holiday in Bray!

July 20th 1959 was a very special day for Aileen. She married Donal Bourke in St. Kevin's Church, Harrington Street. It was the first wedding in the family since Evelyn was married in 1954 but this time we were all invited.

Rachel, only four years old was Aileen's train-bearer and Nuala was Maid of Honour. Aileen looked gorgeous and Donal handsome. Nuala looked lovely and Rachel stole the show in her little ballet shoes, lace gloves and flowing hair, her dress was lovely as well.

It was like belonging to a famous family when we met Eamonn Andrews who was married to Grainne Bourke, Donal's sister. All the men wore top hats and tails including Brian and Terry.

After the photographs, the reception was held in the Four Provinces Dance Hall in Harcourt Street. There was a balcony where the people who attended tea-dances there used to have their afternoon tea away from the dancing. The balcony overlooked the dance floor and Eamonn Andrews walked around making sure we had everything we needed and he brought us lemonade and jelly with ice cream.

In the afternoon he paid for us to go to the pictures. The picture left such an impression on me I can't remember what it was called. I think it was the story of the Family Von Trappe (sub-titled) which was showing on the Corinthian Cinema on Eden Quay, or maybe it was a story with Romy Sneider? Anyway, it was a memorable day. After their marriage Aileen and Donal went to live in Jersey.

Also in the summer of 1959 was the year our daddy took Me, Myra, Enda, Ciaran, Gerald and Rachel with Nuala in charge for a week's holiday to Bray, our first ever holiday away from home. He rented a house with a housekeeper who did the cooking. Apparently the housekeeper liked the boys but was constantly complaining about us girls, nag, nag, nag, it didn't matter what we did or didn't do she complained. But despite that we enjoyed our week there as we liked Bray and so did our daddy.

The days were spent walking along the promenade where the elderly people sat in the sun in deckchairs with blankets over their knees. The wind seemed fresher coming in over the sea. There was the sound of the brass band playing in the bandstand with the sound reaching far and wide. The laughter of children and friendly dogs running along the stony beach. To venture up Bray Head was a walk and a half but worth the climb when reaching the top to view the landscape around.

Those who were old enough to ramble freely enjoyed getting to know Bray village better, because any other time we spent in Bray we were just on the beach gathering stones and paddling with the little fishes gathering around our feet, with the memories of the 'swimming lessons' with daddy.

Bray was well known for its Amusement Arcade and many hours were spent with us having to make big decisions as to what slot machines were worth losing our precious pennies to! We stood for a long time at the glass dome machines with the claw-like crane hands that after the penny was dropped into the money slot. (It was probably a lot more than a penny for that machine), The crane would reach out and hover over the box containing the two shilling bit or the watch, reach down to pick one of them up and drop it into the winning box. I would hold me breath forever but I never won. Still, nothing ventured, nothing.... Chips! well they always tasted better beside the sea.

Myra and me went to the dance in the Legion of Mary hall in the evening, and we left together at the end of the dance even though we had both been asked by our dancing partners if they could walk us back. We were never sure about our daddy's reaction!.

Apart from the nights me daddy was off I was out enjoying meself with me friends being a teenager and hanging around. Nuala was still in charge at home doing everything for everybody and everyone took it all for granted. Everyone knew that Nuala was still seriously thinking of entering the convent. It was still just a question of when.

....

Chapter 71

Where We Spent Our Leisure Days

When we didn't have any money to spend, which was often, we would spend some time in Harold's Cross park. On our way there we would walk over the Grand Canal Bridge where some daring bold children used to swim. It always looked deep and dirty and all kinds of things including dead cats or dogs were thrown in, or so we were told. It also hid stolen dumped bicycles and car tires to name but a few, in it's dark murky depths.

Our route took us past Mount Jerome hospice on one side and the Poor Clare Orphanage and Convent school on the opposite side of the street, where Aileen had gone to school for a year.

As we passed by Mount Jerome hospice I seem to recollect visiting, but me and Myra were told to stand outside the office when Nuala went in with some query or other. While Nuala was gone, Myra and me got a bit bored and tired of doing nothing so we ventured up the Avenue to the hospice.

I am sure we saw nothing even if I said we saw someone lying on a bed with a sheet over their head and it moved, we didn't wait, we ran, we were back where we started before Nuala came out of the office. That adventure was never tried again just in case what we thought we saw just happened to be real!

Harold's Cross It was only a small park with seats in the quiet part for people to sit and read and have their lunch, then a play park with slides and swings but the best part of all was the pond with tadpoles and frogs, the braver of us could be found knee deep in the pond until the park-keeper came along.

Another favourite haunt was to St. Stephen's Green which was close to home and we didn't need to cycle. It was situated at the top of Grafton Street. There was the most wonderful ice cream shop in Cuffe Street on the way and just thinking about the ice cream was mouth watering for more of the same, now lost forever!.

Our mammy used to bring us. It was where every mother with a pram and children, which would have make up a fair size of the Dublin population would spent an afternoon there. St. Stephen's Green was surrounded on four sides by famous places such as The College of

Surgeons, The Shelbourne Hotel, St. Vincent's Hospital and The University Church and not forgetting The Green Cinema (the most famous place of all, to the Donnelly's and every child around!),

    St. Stephen's Green, an oasis of space, two ponds with water fountains, when the wind blew every passerby got soaked and then there was a large duck pond with, a great variety of ducks to be fed, a bridge and rain shelters, a band stand and brass bands entertaining during lunch hours and Sunday afternoons. And landscaped 'Do Not Walk On The Grass' and sculpted flower beds.

....

Chapter 72

A Very Sad Day

Our Granny, whom we all loved even if we were a little afraid of her at times, died on January 28th 1960.

Our Granny was the matriarch of the family and played a central part in all our lives. Every child needs a granny! So her death was a great loss to everyone. I was sixteen years old.

What make it stand out in all our minds was the way we found out. The only dog we ever had was Bobby. On the night - or should I say in the early hours of the morning, when me granny died, his barking woke us all up and we could sense something was wrong as Bobby wouldn't normally bark during the night. Then there was the sound of running footsteps coming down Clanbrassil Street from the direction of O'Donovan's Lane on that cold quiet January morning, to tell us the sad news.

When granny's body was brought to St. Theresa's Church, Donore Avenue, we were standing outside our Granny's house on O'Donovan's Road but me and me younger sisters and brothers were not allowed to attend the service, or attend our Granny's last journey to Mount Jerome Cematry to her final resting place. But Adele, our only cousin, who was the same age as Enda, was allowed: I was always jealous of Adele, because she went everywhere and I didn't and I was older than her!.

Aileen and her husband Donal were still living and working in Jersey when they heard the news. It was such a shock to Aileen that her baby daughter, our first niece, arrived early. Erin made her debut into the world a few days later.

When Sr. Anthony heard the news about the death of granny and the birth of the baby, she asked me if Aileen would call her baby Frances after her grandmother? Erin had already been given her name.

....

Chapter 73

Farewell Nuala

The big day for Nuala and the job vacancy for chief cook, bottle washer and general housekeeper was transferred to me on 3rd October 1960 when the Sisters of Mercy in New Inn, Cashel, Co. Tipperary, welcomed Nuala into their community.

Nuala's new family of 'Sisters' became household names to us. Over the next few years when possible, on big events like Nuala receiving the 'White Veil' then the Black Veil, her 'First Profession' and 'Final Profession' day trips were organized by Brian and a stop at Portlaoise for morning tea was made on the way with everyone looking forward to seeing Nuala again, and talking with the Sisters.

The family were always treated like V.I.P's and the food was a wonderful sight, it was like the family had inherited a new family who were smashing cooks! Nuala was greatly missed by everyone, She had always been there for all the family and had taken great care of us since she was fifteen and a half years old. Life in 100 Lower Clanbrassil Street would never be the same again.

When Daddy and Stella bought a 'Mini' some time later Daddy made day trips to New Inn and the bravest of the family would travel with him. These trips would prove a new experience to the traveler.

Ciaran recalls one such trip: 'On the rare occasion I went to New Inn with daddy driving we took off from home straight up to Leonard's Corner, headed for Harold's Cross Bridge and turned along the canal for the Naas Road. It appeared the traffic lights were on red but daddy was too busy tapping his cigarette out the car window with his right hand, changing gear with his left and steering with his knee to notice. Suffice to say, me and Daddy didn't stop for tea on the way!.

I was left in charge of Rachel aged 6, Gerald aged 10, Ciaran aged 12, Enda aged 13 and Myra aged 15. It was my responsibility to see that they were in school on time in the mornings looking clean and respectable with everything they needed and that they were all in doing their homework at night time when daddy got up to do the night shift at the hotel. The days passed into weeks with all the washing and ironing, darning, sewing, cooking cleaning and shopping.

I used to take Rachel's old pushchair down to Camden Street to do the weekly shopping because it was a lot cheaper in the big shops, and there was a larger variety of food to choose from. I quite enjoyed doing the grocery shopping.

Camden Street, was where Gorovans Drapery Shop and Douglas' Outfitters Shop were and where the 'Providence Vouchers' were accepted and where most of our clothes had been bought over the years. The Communion and Confirmation dresses, coats, underwear, shoes and the boy's suits all came from there.

When I was shopping in Gorovan's I remembered the time Ciaran, when he was a lot younger had gone roaming around while mammy was being served, and he couldn't be found anywhere. Everyone was frantically worried, how could that happen? Where was he? Someone was sent running down to Kevin Street Police Station which was within running distance from Goravan's, to report he was missing and to describe what he was wearing. There was Ciaran sitting with the Gardai eating bread and jam.

Some time later Ciaran admitted he was told he had a habit of getting lost as he recalls a trip to St. Stephen's Green with Nuala, he wasn't holding on to the pram. When they got to the Green he walked straight on and Nuala turned right and bingo, he was lost!. He was found crying and was taken to Kevin Street police station, given a 'Giftie' bar to lick to calm him down and daddy arrived later to bring him home on the crossbar of his bike. Poor Nuala had to return home and announce that she had succeeded in losing Ciaran.

Me being in charge, left me wondering what to do sometimes and Gerald recalls: 'I had to go to bed on me own one dark night, I usually went to bed the same time as Ciaran, but he wasn't there, I don't know where he was.

Deirdre put me to bed, stayed a few minutes, then put off the light and went down stairs. I cried because I was afraid of the dark. Deirdre came up again. In fact she came up twice none too happy and she gets annoyed and I am angry.

On her last traipse up the stairs she produces a matchbox (a bribe!) and in it I find one hae'penny, one Miraculous Medal and a miniature luminous statue of the Virgin Mary. Deirdre tells me to look at the statue in the dark and I won't be afraid. I'm happy!'

During my time 'at home' I made sure there was food in the press, that everyone had clean clothes to wear and that food was on the table. I knew I would never replace Nuala but I did me best. I dressed Rachel for her First Communion and Gerald for his Confirmation. I had great support from Sr. Anthony in Warrenmount who took an interest in what was going on at home and she knew it must have been a bit daunting at times for me.

Nuala was a big act to follow.

As Myra followed me and Enda followed Myra each knew eventually they might have to do their bit in looking after those who were younger. We all took what life threw at us and I got on with being 'the new mother figure' to the family at home for the time being.

••

Chapter 74

Here Is The News in 1961

1) The Munster and Leinster Bank in Baggot Street became a 'Drive in'

2) A young girl of 6 years was rescued from the pond in St. Stephens Green after she fell in while feeding the ducks. Everyone was always surprised it didn't happen more often. There weren't any railings around the pond.

3) There was the problem of people not taking responsibility for their health when everything was being done for them by making Mass X-Ray's available. The truth being, even when people had an X-Ray taken and were diagnosed with TB, if they didn't follow up with the medication, the whole thing was pointless. An appeal to employers to make it compulsory for their staff to take advantage of the service. The 'Church' was also asked to make an appeal to parents.

4) A new arena for Irish Dancing was built by the Corporation in Fairview Park. Árd Craobh had been promoting open-air dancing there for the past two years for the summer evenings. Deirdre and the two Theresas' could vouch for that. They spent happy evenings just as it was getting dark there on their way back from Portmarnock or Malahide on Sunday evenings.

5) A statement was made regarding the teaching of the Irish Language in Secondary schools. That it should hold a place but should not be forced on pupils as some of them leaving Primary Education could barely read or write in the English language and they only had an outline of their religion. 'Life was not as we knew it' when we were on the long road to learning.

6) All is quiet on the streets of Dublin – 'Buses on Strike' – But, people have taken their bicycles out of retirement and some are 'Rusty' and 'Out of Shape'. Cyclists are not aware of car increases and that pedestrians now have 'Right of Way' and should also remember their skills and machines may be a little rusty. Also, lots of things have

changed on the roads since they last cast a leg over the saddle and, pedestrians need to remember that many out-of-retirement cyclists in turn, may think otherwise.

7) A flash from the past - In 1901 the Dublin Gaelic League organized an Irish Language week and held processions through the streets of Dublin in honour of the Language. Limerick had already made March 17th a General Holiday. But March the 17th was not nationally recognized as a holiday until 1903 by a statute of the British Parliament. A great procession organized by the Gaelic League was held in the city to associate the Irish Language and with the idea of honouring St. Patrick by making his Feast Day a National Holiday.

8) When University Students and Official Remunerators were employed to carry out a 'Traffic Census' of cars going over various points in Dublin it became a bone of contention. Protests were made on behalf of unemployed clerical workers who could have benefited with the pay of £2 a shift, also the argument was they could have been employed on the 'Population Census'. The motorists themselves benefited by completing their Traffic Census cards which entitled them to enter into a draw for a cash prize.

9) Freedom of Dublin City was conferred on His Eminence Cardinal Agagarian, Papal Legate – during the Patrician Year Celebrations.

10) The practice of hurling and football on the streets was brought to a stop because of the increase of traffic on the roads. Seven youths were summoned and The Probation Act was applied.

11) At last elocution lessons were recognized as working wonders as 175 competitors took part in the preparatory elocution for girls.

12) A letter of Greeting from the Lord Mayor of Dublin, Mr. Maurice E. Dockrell to the Lord Mayor of Belfast Mr. Robin Kinehan, was brought by pony express. 5 boys and 5 girls aged between 9-13 years were chosen to ride 5 ponies in relay the 110 miles They left from the Mansion House at 8pm and rode through the night to arrive the following morning.

13) The Irish Sugar Company came up with a revolutionary food – Their slogan was 'Just Add Water!'. This idea was introduced at the Spring Show in Ballsbridge, celebrating 130 years. It was the beginning as Ireland took the lead in a bid for a £50m World Market processed food through accelerated freeze drying.

14) Women's Irish Fashion to the Spring Show added colour to an animated scene. It was Bri-Lon Fashion by Sunbeam.

15) April 1961 was confirmed as the wettest month since 1877. (48 years).

16) On the Entertainment Front: The Gaiety Gala opened with Maureen Potter in 'Nuts of May'

And showing at the Olympia Theatre 'Design for a Headstone ' by Seamus Byrne.

At Limerick's Amharclann na Feis : A one night show of Oscar Wilde's Life & Work, 'The Importance of Being Ernest' by Michael MacLiammour.
And, The Gaeity Theatre Concert in aid of the Restoration of Kilmainham Jail was considered a great success by Alan Shepherd.

Chapter 75

Another Wedding

Our big brother Brian met Sheila Scarry while attending the St. Francis Dramatic Society in Harcourt Street and on 26 June 1961 he married Shiela in the Parish Church of St. Nicholas of Myra in Francis Street, which was Sheila's Parish Church.

It was our family's second wedding and of course everyone was invited. I was 17 going on 18 and I was able to wear one of me sewing creations that I'd made in Our Lady's Club Warrenmount and had won a prize.

Their wedding was a grand affair and their reception was held in Power's Hotel, Kildare Street. They were very organized and had bought themselves a house in Palmerstown and were ready to move in when they returned from their Honeymoon in Galway. Their first daughter Áine was born on the 3rd April 1962.

Me social life continued in the evenings with the same friends I knew from me short working life. We went dancing, walking and cycling together. I did keep in touch with a few other friends though they had stayed on at school and were studying. I was still a member of the Club in Warrenmount.

Daddy was still in the same job as Night Porter and would come home every morning with the same question: 'Are you alright?'

What could I say? I could not see a future before me, all I could visualise was a lifetime of being at home looking after everyone. Terry was now the only older person still at home taking on the role of being Boss but he was out at work all day and enjoying his social life.

When Terry was at home and daddy was either in bed or out, Terry wasn't short of giving me a clip around the ear if I answered him back for whatever reason. I threatened to stop darning his socks when he did that. In fact what I said to him was 'I'm going to tell Daddy on you and you can darn your own bloody socks!'

And flung the sock at him darning needle and all!

Another year passed and I was still at home. Daddy was still asking the same question to which there was really no answer.

But I must at some time have given it a lot of thought because it wouldn't have been normal to be content being at home doing mundane things all day, not working or earning a wage and not being with people me own age, but what choice did I have?

I had spent some time thinking about what the possibilities might be out there in the big world but I had not a clue how to go about making them happen. I was stuck in a rut and not even me mind was free thinking. But there came a day when I was attending a Retreat and there I was present at an early Mass when a visiting Sister of Mercy, Sr. Ethel made an appeal for young girls to look within their hearts and see if God was calling them to work for the conversion of those who had no Faith. Well, as I sat there it was like everything and everyone in the Oratory melted into nothingness and there was only Sr. Ethel, she was talking to me. I became all excited and could see meself as being the Saviour of Souls on a Pagan Island, what a challenge! I did have a very vivid imagination!.

I flew the short distance back home after Mass as though on Angels' Wing's as I realised 'Yes, Yes' that's what I want and I needed to talk with me daddy.

He just said 'Is that what you really want?'

I said, 'Yes' and the wheels started rolling.

The interviews began, of which there were many, but finally with the required packed suitcase of everything in either the colour navy, black or white, as I was entering the Convent as an Aspirant and not as a Postulant. We were set to go. There were three other girls from Dublin and Sr. Ethel, so I got the window seat on the airplane, I sat on me own and I was fascinated watching the clouds float by just outside the window.

After six months I made my first trip back to Dublin and returned to Guernsey with a suitcase packed with nearly everything in black, it was felt I was ready to become a Postulant. I began a life of prayers, many, many rules, the ringing of bells, early morning meditation, hard work and more prayers, Chanting the Office three or four times daily and I was back studying in a class with school pupils, a school world I thought I'd left behind when I finished secondary education!. Six months later I received the White Veil. Within two months I knew the life as a nun was not for me. I became ill and unhappy. It was time to go home.

I had spent fourteen months away from Dublin with only the one very short visit back, but all the time I was away I constantly wondered what on earth was I doing and surely life at home must have changed and probably everyone was having a great time and missing me terribly because in my own way I was missing them.

During the time I was away Daddy, Betty, Stella and their friend Patsy decided it would be nice to visit and be there when I received the

White veil and we all spent a few days walking on the beaches and getting to know the Island, which was very beautiful. There were many wonderful cliffs walks as well and the heather growing on the side of the cliffs was a wonderful sight. Daddy, Betty, Stella and Patsy stayed in the bungalow quite near to where I was staying so we saw a lot of each other. It was lovely being with them and the Sisters at Blanchelande College were very welcoming.

It was during that visit daddy took me aside and told me that me Mammy had been found but that she didn't want to 'come home'. Daddy had been contacted because mammy was having an operation and had put daddy's name as next of kin. Apparently when Mammy had left home on December 4th 1957 she had gone by train to Belfast looking for a job but couldn't get one so she went from Belfast to Liverpool and vanished into the crowds. She had been living in England since then. That was possibly one of the reasons the police were never able to locate her as their first steps were to watch the Sea Ports of the North Wall and Dun Laoghaire.

On the evening of November 22nd 1963 I was packing me bag when the news came on the television that The President of the United States of America, John F. Kennedy, had been assassinated in Dallas, Texas. The world was in shock! The children in the college were in tears and a special Mass was said. I was having supper in the Refectory with the other Sisters.

Very early the next morning in the aftermath of that tragedy which happened worlds away from where I was, I sat in the airport. I was alone. It was 7.30 am. The Channel Islands were shrouded in fog and flights were grounded. The flight had touched town in Jersey to wait for clearance to complete it's journey to Dublin.

I had very little money, but I bought a copy of every newspapers and filled in the long hours while waiting for the fog to clear, I read each paper from cover to cover to make sense of the tragic events. There was a strange quietness about everything. Suddenly the fog lifted, we were rushed on to the plane and I did finally arrive in Dublin sometime in the afternoon. Me daddy was waiting for me.

···

Chapter 76

Home Again

While I had been away Rachel had been staying with Brian and Sheila. Daddy, Ciaran and Gerald went to visit her for her Birthday and brought her presents of a tea set and a telephone.

Rachel recalls her Christmas with them. She was eight years old and she received the most wonderful doll's ranch complete with furniture and a roof that lifted off. It was only when she saw the house had the same wallpaper that Brian and Sheila had on their living room walls she realized that Brian had made it and that it hadn't come from Santa.

Myra had started at Trinity College and was looking after things at home. Enda was close to finishing school and Ciaran and Gerald had qualified to be teenagers but were still attending Synge Street School.

Ciaran and Gerald were quite close to each other during their school years and they looked out for each other. It was around this time when Ciaran happened to be the only one at home when Gerald began having severe pains when his appendix burst, although they didn't know that was the cause at the time.

Ciaran helped Gerald up to the HCR Chemist at Leonard's Corner, the pharmacist suggested he bring Gerald to see the doctor on South Circular Road, who then told them to go straight to the hospital. So there they were struggling along the South Circular Road with Gerald bent double and in a lot of pain and Ciaran helping as best he could.

A kind motorist stopped and gave them a lift to the Meath Hospital. Ciaran reckoned the lift probably saved Gerald's life!

Now that I was back home Rachel returned home as well. I had a feeling Daddy was going to ask me to take over again but I said 'No'. I needed to get a job and have a life of me own.

Within six weeks of my returning home to Clanbrassil Street an old flame of mine turned up on the doorstep. We went walking out together again. We had only gone out with each other for three months when I was seventeen and he was sixteen when he told me he couldn't afford me any more. So here he was again, he had just heard I'd been away and that now I was back.

There was a scarcity of jobs and no money. I asked daddy if I could have some 'Providence Vouchers' so I could buy suitable clothes for interviews (wishful thinking). I had absolutely no experience at doing anything and I wasn't too keen on saying I had just come out of a Convent, so lied and boasted about all the experience I'd gained working in a similar shop in Jersey. I got a job in Liptons of Moore Street and with all the experience I said I had, I couldn't tell the difference between a back rasher, a gammon rasher or a streaky rasher or what the difference was between pork or beef sausages or the different cheeses on offer.

I'd stand at the shop window let me hand hover over the loose meats in the display window until the customer made their choice. I had told the manager that where I last worked everything had been sold pre-packed.

I enjoyed the job but lost it a few months later because I couldn't get to work on time. The manager was such a nice man he gave me a good reference and they all said they'd miss me. I had unfortunately arrived in late on the very day the shop owners were visiting. That was me downfall!.

From there and clutching me good reference I was fortunate to get a job in the new Power's Supermarket in North Earl Street and was there when they were getting the counters fixed and supply deliveries to stack on the shelves.

At the grand opening there was a rush of customers and the money poured into the cash tills but not to the staff. The wages were not great but it was a job. The job proved to be quite boring wrapping cheese in cling-film, Stacking shelves and arranging the cold food in display cabinets.

When the shop got very busy I was promoted to the position as 'floor-walker'. I had to pretend to be a customer and keep an eye out for people shoplifting. I soon learnt how nifty some were with their many 'hidden pockets' inside their coats where they slipped their unpaid items when they thought no-one was looking and then paid for just one or two items at the check-out.

Then I was transferred to their new branch in Henry Street. I was put on the slowest cash till ever and me trying to impress – so unsuccessfully: it didn't work. I didn't get promoted even though promises were made or hinted at.

Everyone worked long hours in the Supermarket from Monday to Saturday with a half day on Wednesdays. I had a friend who was ill who was a patient in Ballyowen, so for a few weeks during the summer, as soon as I'd had me lunch I would cycle out to visit her. We would spend a couple of hours chatting and playing table tennis before it was time for me to leave.

Ballyowen was just a short distance beyond where Brian, his wife

Sheila and their daughter Áine was living so I would call into their place for tea and spend some time with them and sometimes play with Áine if she was still up. It was a nice break before the journey home.

I would leave at about ten o'clock at night when it was getting dark. All through the summer I made the trip and enjoyed it. I never had any bother on the road and I always felt safe, until….

One night I was cycling home when I became aware there was someone riding a motorbike behind me. As I cycled it kept pace behind me. When I stopped, it stopped, and so it went on for quite sometime. I was afraid to turn around so I continued on keeping the same pace.

Then the motorbike pulled along side me just as I was leaving Arran Quay to cross the bridge into Bridge Street. It was a police motorbike. I stopped when he stopped.

'Why didn't you stop when you heard me behind you?' He asked me.

'I thought you were a stranger trying to get me and I was afraid' I said.

Then he just said 'And where is your back light?'

'Oh, I forgot it, I wasn't expecting to be this late' I lied.

'Well make sure you have it the next time, it's the law." And then as an after-thought he said 'By the way what's your name?' I told him. He then said 'Any news of your mammy?'

I was flummoxed.

Chapter 77

A Wedding Abroad

Now everyone took his or her rightful turn in the family and with Aileen and Brian married it was now Terry's turn.

While I was away, Terry was working in Jersey where Aileen and Donal were running a hotel but he came back to Dublin before he left for England.

He'd been working in England for some time as a commercial traveler and on a visit to Dublin he broke the news to all that he was engaged to a girl from Manchester. Can you imagine how surprised we all were when shortly after his return to Manchester he wrote to say he was getting married. We are talking about me shy handsome brother that I thought butter wouldn't melt in his mouth!

Now that Wedding was an event and a half. Terry and his future bride Judy York were married on 26 August 1964 in her home town in Manchester, England. We were all of course invited and it would be the only overseas marriage we would attend travelling by boat.

We travelled on the night boat from Dun Laoghaire to Liverpool and then by train to Manchester. The boat was crowded so after making a tour around the boat to make sure we knew where the toilets were, we found space on the floor on the deck outside. We were too excited to sleep. It was a lovely warm night but I felt a little queezy from the movement of the waves and the rocking of the boat. It felt like the journey would never end, but we survived.

For most of us it was our first time on a boat and our first time visiting England. We'd heard lots of stories about England and that the streets were paved with gold, it must have been London they were talking about because we didn't come across any gold on the streets in Manchester, but the idea of visiting it well it didn't seem possible but there we were on a boat heading that way.

Everyone was booked into a small family Guest House for Bed and Breakfast and we felt very important being served breakfast of Orange Juice, cereal and a fry and we weren't expected to wash up afterwards!

After we girls went to have our hair done by the local hairdresser and dressed in our finery specially bought for the occasion and the boys in their new suits, we walked to the Parish Church which was close by.

It was quite a nervous time for everyone as none of us had met Judy or her family and visa-versa. Judy only had two sisters and no brothers but although not all of us were at the wedding, there were quite a few of us there. We were all on our best behaviour and watched the Marriage ceremony with interest.

In those days if it was a mixed marriage the couple could not be married at the High Altar and as Judy's religion was Church of England the priest led Terry and Judy to a Side Altar where they were joined together as man and wife.

Judy's mother became a little anxious when she saw the priest leading Terry and Judy away from the main Altar and she got all her guests to follow them. Terry and Judy didn't have a nuptial Mass but a Blessing: it was a very meaningful occasion.

I certainly couldn't remember many of the guests except Judy's mother and father and her younger sister Hilary. Rachel and Hilary seem to get on and Hilary was invited to visit everyone in Dublin.

Judy's mammy was a little wary of our family as she didn't know that we were actually very nice people. She'd got the impression that most of the Irish were part of the IRA and nothing good could come from marrying an Irishman. Judy later said it took her mother a long time to get to know Terry but she did eventually grow to be really fond of him!

Judy later recalled that she had wished herself and Terry had eloped. She felt so self-conscious. She found meeting the family a bit overwhelming. She met Terry through her best friend Christine Lloyd who had told her there were some really nice Irish men who had just arrived in England who enjoyed Folk Singing and she loved folk singing as well. Judy met Terry in an Irish Club called The Wild Geese in Withington, and that's where Judy learnt a lot more of the Irish Ballads.

Judy thought Aileen was smart and sophisticated, that Gerald was a gorgeous little shy thing and that Ciaran kept having a go at her accent. The rest of us didn't seem to leave any lasting impression on her. I believe everyone enjoyed the wedding, I certainly did.

Judy got to know everyone when she came back to Dublin for a visit with Terry when they brought their first daughter Lynne with them to meet us all. They stayed with Betty and Stella who had bought a new double bed especially for them, they only found that out later. It was so like Betty and Stella not to make a fuss. It was the first time we heard the word 'naughty' being used instead of 'bold' when Lynne was doing something she shouldn't have been doing in the garden.

Judy remembered daddy's driving skills and recalls the terror she felt when she couldn't relax enough to enjoy all the wonderful sights but loved the beautiful Terraces and Georgian doors just as daddy did.

She said that Dublin felt quite different to England, more foreign than she expected but she loved and enjoyed her visits, the atmosphere and the music in the pubs. She wanted very much to be accepted by the 'Donnelly Clan' knowing she was the first non-Irish in the family.

Judy recalls a particular drive in the famous 'Mini' being driven by Daddy when Pearse and Doris went along for the drive. Doris, being her usual tactless self remarked out loud that there weren't any views in England to match those of Ireland. Doris didn't realize at the time how close she came to being pushed off the cliff they were standing on at the time, says Judy

Then there was the day visit to Nuala in New Inn. (Nuala was then wearing the long black habit) and Judy noticed how much attention Nuala gave Lynne. She became Judy's friend for life!

While Rachel was still young and mammy had been gone a while Daddy and her became companions. They went to the cinema quite often so Rachel could boast of seeing the films 'The Long, The Short and The Tall', 'Fiddler on the Roof', 'Krakatoa' and 'The Sound of Music' in the Cinerama Cinema in Talbot Street, to name but a few.

They went on trips together in the Mini that daddy shared with Stella. They would go visiting Synotts in Ashford and Woodbridge on Sundays to hear Uncle Frank Donnelly play Honky Tonk Piano and Mick O'Dwyer play the Banjo.

With Daddy and the Mini, Rachel enjoyed their trips around Kerry, and especially Killarney. Daddy loved Killarney, and Dan Lowries in particular.

Doris also recalls many happy musical evenings in Synge Street where Daddy used to play the violin, Frank and Pearse took turns on the piano. Julianne who was a member of our Lady's Choral Society, had a wonderful singing voice and was the vocal accompaniment

Rachel heard by accident that she was going to join Nuala in New Inn. No, not as a nun, but as a pupil. Myra and Enda thought she was asleep while they were talking about it. Inwardly Rachel was quite excited about it and watched as her suitcase filled with new clothes, blankets, sheets and a counterpane that she had no idea what it was, it was just a posh name for a bedspread, everything else that she might need was put into it also. Because we didn't have two sheets to sleep between at home Rachel didn't know what to do with hers when she got to New Inn so she put the spare sheet under her pillow.

Anyone who called at the house or visited was expected to admire her 'Trouseau'. Ciaran and Gerald delighted in teasing her by singing 'They're coming to take you away, Ha Ha!'

Chapter 78

Change of Jobs

After a year and broken promises of promotion I decided it was time to look for another job.

I had no problem getting a job in a chemist on the South Circular Road for a year. It was much closer to home and I could walk there so I was never late. That proved to be a very good year. I was working with an elderly pharmacist who was delighted to have help in the shop. I learnt to love going to work and meeting new people every day and being allowed to dress the shop window with all the Christmas items. Health-wise it was a good year with having access to all the health supplements.

After about a year I was transferred to the owner's Chemist on the Quays and put in charge of his other branch in Tara Street.

All went well and I was quite content working between the two chemists and going on various courses to learn how to apply make-up to encourage customers to use it. That was strange for me because I never used make up.

Then me boss thought it was OK for his children to come around and mess up me window displays, moving things around and leaving sticky sweets in all the wrong places and chewing gum stuck underneath the counters. Of course I kept complaining and telling them off so their eldest sister complained to her daddy and I was fired on Christmas Eve. The future didn't look too bright.

It wasn't an excellent Christmas with that hanging over me, but such as life. In a way I was a little relieved because the time I spent in the chemist in Tara Street on me own some shady characters were hanging around and one or two of them were coming in too often and making me feel a little uncomfortable. No, I didn't feel uncomfortable when one customer asked me if I sold 'French Letters'. I was so naïve I didn't have a clue about what he was asking for. I rang me boss on Eden Quay and he suggested I tell them to ask a sailor at the North Wall or enquire at the local Post Office. That customer left the shop laughing.

Any New Year is not the time to be looking for work. There was nothing in the papers as business was slow even in the supermarkets. There were one or two jobs advertised in the areas around Sutton and

Portmarnock on the north side of Dublin. A long way from where I lived but me need was great, I had no money.

The first interview I got was with a firm in Sutton, but they said I was over qualified. That was the first time any one had ever accused me of being 'over' anything. I wasn't sure whether to be delighted or sad, that didn't put money in me pocket. I tried a few others jobs advertised but they were still too far away to get to by bicycle at 8.30am every morning.

I finally settled for a job in Phillips Factory, Finglas: an excellent manufacturer of quality electrical goods. I found meself back on an assembly line making coils for their radios and televisions. I had come full circle, I was now back in the same situation I had been in when I had left school. The same noise, the radio blaring, the bad language but this time it was the filthy jokes being told by the girls to the men and this really upset me because I had moved on from days like that. I spent some time crying in silence over the next couple of weeks and secretly wishing I was somewhere else. This wasn't really where I wanted to be, but needs be, here I was and it was time to join the Union .

I stayed on the factory floor but never felt comfortable and had secret visions of working in the glass surrounded, open-plan offices on the first floor. 'Some Day' I would say to meself and it seemed like some miracle had happened somewhere when one of the floor managers took me aside and asked me if I would like to work in the office upstairs, there was a vacancy for an office clerk.

Someone somewhere had waved the magic wand. I tried not to sound too delighted with meself as there were one or two other girls there who had mentioned to me they wouldn't mind getting a job up there so I felt I was the lucky one.

I had to relinquish me white coat which I had made me own by writing me name along both lapels in large green water-proof felt tip marker letters. The housecoat would be of no use to any other of the staff unless their name was Deirdre!

I was requested to cancel me membership with the Union and it was decided me lunch time would be changed so I was not on the same break as the people I had worked with on the assembly line.

I was very happy with me new status. I went for more typing classes in the local Technical College and the firm paid because there was a telex machine in the office to communicate with their partner company in Holland with correspondence about the various 'baby coils' and other equipment I didn't know much about.

All the office updates, sales and orders and the personal news items announcing the news of a new baby daughter to the Boss and his wife, were sent via Telex. The thing about using the telex to send messages was it wasn't built so messages could be corrected if mistakes were made, before sending each telex and telexes were quite expensive to send. I learnt about office procedure and enjoyed the humour that went on with the office staff.

There was a school leaver who joined the staff as a junior who was about sixteen years old but the other male staff gave him a hard time. They thought they were being funny but he didn't think so. Then one day he snapped and told the boss he would some day be big enough to get his own back. This threat did not go down well with his boss and the young lad was embarrassed with his outburst. The young lad did blossom into a fine young man and was never challenged again in the office: well not while I was there.

Everyone had to clock in and out so it was important to be on time. It was me first step to doing a job I liked. I remember someone asking me if I would ever like to work in an office when I was still at school. I had said 'No thank you, office work sounds like a very boring job, just sitting at a desk all day'. I then realized it was anything but boring!

••

Chapter 79

To Have And To Hold

Now I had a steady job and earning a good wage and Jimmy me boyfriend, was working also, so we decided to make plans to get married. We got engaged first and we each splashed out for new clothes to celebrate the occasion and Jimmy bought me a heart shaped diamond engagement ring. It was a very happy day and it wasn't long before we started making wedding plans.

We did all the right things. We attended the six evening sessions of the pre-marriage course because it was hinted we would learn how to make things for the home, and the Facts of Life. etc. Now you may think that's a bit … but to be honest, I really didn't know everything I needed to know. That was why we attended really. How naïve we were!

We booked an appointment with the Parish Priest at St. Kevin's Parish Church on the South Circular Road for the Banns to be read and to discuss the Wedding Mass, even though we had asked Fr. Sylvius C.P. from Mount Argus, a very good friend of ours, to perform the Wedding Ceremony. We booked the Power Hotel in Kildare Street for the reception. It had been recommended to me by me brother Brian.

We ordered the Cake, the flowers and the white shoes for Enda who was to be me Bridesmaid. Jimmy had already asked his friend Tommy Henderson to be his best man. Tommy married Alice, his fiancé the following day. Me friend Noeleen Urell, who was an excellent tailoress who made beautiful clothes, offered to make me wedding dress, Enda's bridesmaid dress and me 'Going Away' suit, a coat with matching dress and hat. Meself and Noeleen had remained friends since our school days.

As Jimmy was the youngest son in his family and the only one now living with his mammy in Harold's Cross she didn't take too kindly to the news that he was getting married, she was losing her baby son!. There was no mention from his Mammy that she was delighted to be gaining a daughter!. Jimmy was twenty two years old and old enough to marry without his mammy's permission. His father who was a policeman had died when Jimmy was twelve years old. His mammy did offer to pay for the Honeymoon as me daddy was paying for the wedding reception.

The real problems began when the wedding lists were being drawn up and there were lots of friends his mammy wanted to invite but there was a limited number of places so things became a little uncomfortable between me and me future mother in law. We came to an understanding in the end.

A few days before the wedding and gifts began to arrive and it looked like there wasn't enough room in the house in Clanbrassil Street to display the wedding presents and enjoy a 'Hen's Night', I asked Betty and Stella for the use of their place just for one evening. They said that would be fine.

They were then let into the secret of other occasions unbeknownst to them that '21 O'Donovan Road' was considered the safest place to go when any of us were having an evening out dancing or had missed the last bus and couldn't get back home before the bewitching hour of 11pm when the front door of our Clanbrassil Street address was locked. Or if our daddy was working that night and no amount of knocking or shouting could arouse anyone but the neighbours, the bravest ones would walk to 'O'Donovan Road', climb in through the parlour window and spend the night there, leaving early in the morning before anyone was up. This was because the front window in our house was shielded by a railing with spikes. The climbers risked having their clothes torn, but it was attempted many a time with success.

On Easter Tuesday, February 28th 1967 early in the morning Myra, Enda and me went to the hairdresser's on Harcourt Street and each of us came home with new hair creations of our choice for this special day. Rachel was home from school for the Easter Holidays. Enda's new white shoes didn't arrive on time but she was quite happy to wear her black shoes and no one noticed, they were all too busy admiring themselves and each other.

Noeleen came to dress me in her creation of white. All was ready. The car was waiting at the door, the neighbours were all there wishing me luck and we, daddy, Enda and me were driven the short distance to the church.

As I was heading towards the main entrance to the church with me arm linking me daddy's arm the previous couple had just left and the red carpet they had hired for their wedding was being rolled up before I could make me grand entrance and journey down the centre aisle towards me future husband and the main Altar. Not having a red carpet didn't mean not having a first class wedding. The Wedding ceremony was perfect.

Then followed the taking of photos, dozens of them from every angle with every group and it was not warm outside but we all smiled as requested by the photographer.

Then we got into the car for the journey to see Sr. Anthony and the Sisters in Warrenmount. to receive a blessing from them, and give our guests time to arrive at the hotel before us. There was a flurry of snow as we stepped into the wedding car which was beautifully warm.

The Hotel did us proud and we would have recommended it to everyone. The wedding tables were tastefully set and everyone seemed happy with the seating arrangements, if they weren't we didn't hear about it. The hotel food tasted fantastic and the drinks flowed. Everything was just right except that Nuala didn't have permission to attend the Wedding Mass or the breakfast so neither did Betty or Stella, but they did stop by and came in while the wedding breakfast was in full swing, they stayed a few minutes to wish us every happiness and to meet a few people that they may not have met otherwise.

We left the hotel about 5pm that evening for a flight to Liverpool where we spent the first night of our Honeymoon in a hotel near the Airport. That whole night was a nightmare to us. We guessed the hotel staff knew we were honeymooners and every half hour or so through the night someone would rattle the door handle, then a whispered 'Sorry' when they found the chain on the door. We didn't think it was funny but they must have. We were too shy to say anything before we left the next day.

In the morning we took a quick tour around the city and the many places the 'Beatles' had sung about. We caught a late flight to the Island of Guernsey where we spent our honeymoon in a Guest House named 'Le Jardin des Fleurs' where the proprietor thought she should bring us up a cup of tea in bed every morning, much against my protest. I was not amused, I didn't feel comfortable about someone else seeing us both in bed, even if we were married!. I was such a prude!

....